OBJECT LESSONS FROM NATURE

JOANNE E. DE JONGE

BAKER BOOK HOUSE
Grand Rapids, Michigan 49516

ISBN: 0-8010-2989-9

Second printing, March 1990

Contents

Introduction

Children take a special delight in the little things of creation. They're fascinated by ants, spiders, worms, rocks, flowers, even twigs, and react to these with a sense of wonder seldom seen in adults.

The lessons in this book appeal to children's delight and fascination by using natural objects often ignored by adults. Each lesson enhances the children's sense of wonder and brings them closer to their Creator by highlighting a biblical truth.

The objects themselves are easily found, usually right outside your front door. In a few cases of more obscure creatures, suggestions on where to find them are given and alternatives are listed.

To aid you throughout the year, the lessons are arranged in seasonal order. The first seventeen lessons (through "Secure in the Lord") use objects which can be found in the dead of winter, or anytime throughout the year. Lesson 18 ("Signs of the Seasons") uses an object found in the spring, and from there the lessons proceed through summer and fall, to Lesson 38, best used in November. The final fifteen lessons are designed for special days, with objects readily available anytime of the year.

Because every person has an individual style of presentation, these lessons are suggestions, and can be easily altered to suit your style. Each lesson, however, can be given exactly as written, since it is presented in conversational form and includes "stage directions." In a few cases, several suggestions of presentation are given. In all cases, Scriptures quoted are taken from the New International Version of the Bible.

Now that you know the design of this book, take a few minutes to page through it and read around in it. I hope that you find, in the perusing and using of these lessons, you and the adults who "listen in," begin to take a special delight in the little things of creation along with the children. And through that special delight in creation, may all involved feel a deeper appreciation of the Creator.

1

Honor Your Parents

Scripture: Children, obey your parents in the LORD, for this is right. "Honor your father and mother"—which is the first commandment with a promise—"that it may go well with you and that you may enjoy long life on the earth" (Eph. 6:1–3).

Theme: God told us to obey our parents because he loves us.

Object: A spider plant with several "babies" (young plants) hanging from it.

I'd like your help with this plant. I want to cut off some of these little plants [or "babies"] and put them in pots, but I'm not sure they're ready. You can help me decide.

Right now, everything that the little plants need to grow comes from the big plant through these runners. *(Point out the runners that attach the small plants.)* Each little plant must stay on the big plant until it has roots of its own. If I cut a little plant off before it has roots, it might die.

(Separate an immature "baby" without rootlets from the others and hold it by the runner so the children can see it.) Does this have any roots? *(Pause for response.)* I don't see any. Should I cut this off? *(Shake your head to elicit the right response.)* I'd better leave it on; it still needs the big plant.

Let's try another one. *(If you have another immature "baby.")* Do you see any little roots? Is this ready for life on its own? *(Pause for response).* I doubt it. It should stay with the big plant and grow a bit yet.

Maybe I should let the small plants grow a bit yet, what do you think? *(Pause for response).* They're doing very well attached to the big plant. God has a good plan here; the parent plant *(Point out the big plant.)* helps the young ones grow strong and healthy. Let's not cut them off too soon.

Did you ever compare yourself to a plant? The Bible talks about God's people well planted. But, to be well planted, what do you need? *(Point to the rootless "babies.")* Roots! You have to grow some roots before you can stand on your own.

Right now you're like one of these little plants, and your parents are this big plant. You're growing little roots; you're learning right from wrong, how to take care of yourself, and how to grow in Jesus. But you have a long way to go yet, don't you? You don't want to be cut off from that big plant, do you? Just like these little plants, you're not ready for that.

God has a plan for your life, just as he does for this plant. He wants you to grow strong and healthy in all ways. So he gave you parents to help you learn about life and become a good, strong Christian.

And he gave you a rule to live by. He said, "Children, obey your parents in the LORD, for this is right."

You know why he gave you that rule, don't you? In his own words, he said, "That it may go well with you. . . ." He loves you, he wants only what's best for you. Right now, your parents know what's best. That's why God said, "Obey your parents."

Thanks for helping me with this plant. I won't cut the "babies" off yet. They should stay with the big plant to grow healthy; just like you should obey your parents, to grow into strong, healthy Christians.

2

Stumbling Block or Stepping-Stone?

Scripture: Matthew 21:42–44
"The stone the builders rejected has become the capstone . . ." (Matt. 21:42).

Theme: Jesus can be either a stumbling block or a stepping-stone in your Christian life.

Object: A rock large enough for a child to stand on. (If children come to the front of the church, place the rock so that some of the children must either walk around it or over it.)

I've put a big rock right here, where people walk. Some of you couldn't miss that rock could you? You had to step over it or walk around it, if you came down here to the front. It's simply too big to ignore.

Pretend for a minute that this rock is so big, it fills that whole center aisle. You have to walk down that aisle, and the rock is in the way. What are you going to do?

You could ignore the rock, pretend you don't see it— but then you might stub your toe, like this. *(Demonstrate.)* Or you might even stumble over it, like this. *(Demonstrate.)* You might hurt yourself by ignoring that rock. It would be a real stumbling block.

What else could you do with the rock? *(Pause for re-*

sponse.) Yes, you could use it as a stepping-stone. You could climb over it. You could even stand on it and be taller than you are now.

That rock was a stumbling block for me. Who would like to make it a stepping-stone? *(Pick a volunteer. Help him/her stand up on the rock.)*

Now this rock is good for ___[name]___ . It's helping him/her stand taller and see more than before. This rock can help you in other ways, too. Pretend that, for some strange reason, the church started flooding, and there was water in all the aisles. Who would have dry feet? *(Pause for response.)* Or if someone's chasing you, climb up on the rock, and you're a bit taller and have an advantage. This rock can be a very good thing. *(Help the child off the rock.)*

Jesus is like a rock in our lives. He's there and he's too big to ignore. What are we going to do about him?

We could try to ignore him, but then he'll be a stumbling block. We'll be trying to live a life without God.

Or we can accept him as a stepping-stone, a rock to stand on. We can learn about him, pray to him, and try to live like he wants us to live. And then he'll help us stand tall, see things clearly, and fight off our troubles.

What is Jesus going to be to you, a stumbling block or a stepping-stone? He wants to be the most important stepping-stone in your life.

3

If Rocks Could Talk

Scripture: Luke 19:37–40
"I tell you," he replied, "if they keep quiet, the stones
will cry out" (Luke 19:40).

Theme: God wants us to praise him aloud.

Objects: Several rocks in a bag.

I've brought a bag of rocks with me today. *(Pile
the rocks in front of the children.)* Look at them. They don't
do anything; they don't move; they don't breathe;
they're not growing; and they certainly don't say anything. They just sit there, still and silent.

Imagine for a minute that these rocks could talk.
What do you suppose they would say? Maybe, "Move
over, you're squashing me," or, "Don't put me back in
that bag," or "Give me air"? I don't think so.

If these rocks could talk, I know what they'd say.
They'd say something like "Praise God!" or "All glory
to God!" or "Jesus is King!"

How do I know that? Jesus said so! Long ago, he said
that if people didn't shout and sing his praises, rocks
would cry out instead.

Jesus was riding into Jerusalem on a donkey, and
there was a crowd of people around him, making a fuss
over him. They were shouting things like "Blessed is the

king who comes in the name of the LORD!" and "Peace in heaven and glory in the highest!" The Bible says that they were joyfully praising God in loud voices.

There were some people in the crowd who didn't like all that noise and shouting. They were the kind of people who like everything all prim and proper, and get upset if you don't act the way they want you to. They didn't like the crowd praising God so loudly, so they told Jesus to make his disciples be quiet. That's when Jesus said, "If they keep quiet, the stones will cry out."

In other words, Jesus was saying that God likes to have people praising him aloud. And if people ever stop praising him, he'll let the rocks sing out.

I don't think these rocks are going to stand up and holler right now. It certainly would be sad if they did. That would mean that we've stopped praising God.

Do you think that God is a wonderful God? Are you glad that Jesus came to save you? Do you love him? Then don't be afraid to say so. Never be shy about singing, saying, or even shouting God's praises. That's what he wants us to do.

Let's all praise God, aloud, as much as we can. Let's make sure that these rocks never have to talk.

4

The Salt of the Earth

Scripture: "You are the salt of the earth . . ." (Matt. 5:13).

Theme: Salt is essential for life; it also preserves and flavors. We can be like salt in helping to bring the Word of Life to others; we should also try to preserve and flavor the world for God.

Objects: A salt block or part of one, a piece of beef jerky, a saltshaker.

Look at the three things I have with me today, and see if you can tell me how they're alike. *(Show them the salt block, saltshaker, and beef jerky.)* They don't look much alike, but the first two can give you a clue: a *salt* block and a *salt*shaker. Any ideas? *(Pause for response.)* Yes, all three of these have salt in them.

This block is almost pure salt. If I set it outside for a while, some animals probably would find it and lick it. Animals need salt, so they will lick on salt or something salty wherever they can find it. We need salt too. In fact we would die without salt.

Sometimes we like to shake a little extra salt on our food—but not too much! *(Hold up saltshaker.)* Can you imagine what an egg would taste like without salt? Besides keeping us alive, salt helps flavor our foods.

Salt also keeps food from spoiling. *(Hold up beef jerky.)* That's why this beef jerky is good, although it may be

13

over a year old. Someone rubbed salt into it, and the salt helped keep it good.

So salt is very important in three ways. It helps keep us alive; it keeps food from spoiling; and it adds flavor to food.

Jesus knew how important salt was. In fact he once talked about it. He said, "You are the salt of the earth." What do you think he meant?

Well, think about salt for a minute. We just said that salt helps keep us alive. There are people in the world who are dying right now. Their bodies are okay, but their souls are dying because they don't know Jesus.

What can you do about that? *(Pause for response.)* That's right, you can tell them about Jesus! That way, you can be salt for their souls. You can help their souls to live.

We also said that salt keeps food from spoiling or going bad. Jesus wants you to act like salt by keeping your little part of the world good in his eyes.

How can you do that? Well, pretend that one of your friends wants you to do something bad. Maybe, tease someone that has no friends. Would you do that? *(Pause for response.)* Of course not! You'd try to do what's right. That will keep your little part of the world good, the same way salt keeps food good.

What could you say to someone who wants you to do something bad? *(Pause for response.)* That's right! You can say that Jesus wants you to be good. And when you talk like that, you're being salt, adding the flavor of Jesus to life around you. You're sprinkling him into your conversation, just like sprinkling salt on food.

There are lots of ways you can be salt. You can flavor your life with talk about Jesus. You can keep your corner of the world good by doing what he wants you to do. And you can bring life to others by telling them about Jesus.

In whatever you do, Jesus wants *you* to be the salt of the earth.

5

One Body, Many Parts

Scripture: Now you are the body of Christ, and each one of you is a part of it (1 Cor. 12:27).

Theme: Although we are all different, each one of us is important in Christ's church and has an individual contribution to make.

Object: None to take with you. Use a child as a volunteer.

I need a volunteer today, someone to stand up here beside me. *(Choose the volunteer and have him/her stand next to you.)*

I want the rest of you to take a long look at ___[name]___ and tell me what's the most important part of his/her body. Is it his/her heart? Lungs? Eyes? What do you think? *(Pause for responses.)*

(Answer according to responses given, pointing out the necessity of each, but how it can't function alone. Examples below.)

His/her heart? No one can live without a heart to pump blood, but what if he/she had no blood? That's important, too. Her/his eyes? *(Cover the child's eyes.)* Now _____ can't see where he/she is going, but suppose he/she had no feet to get there? _____ could always feel the way. His/her brain? That's right, nothing would work without the brain. But what if _____ had a brain but no lungs? Would he/she live?

15

I think you get my point. There's really not one most important part. Every part of _____'s body is important for some reason. Thanks, _____. You may sit down now.

That's exactly the way it is with Christians. The Bible tells us that we are the body of Christ and each one of us is a part of it. That doesn't mean that we're a part of the body that Jesus had when he was on earth. It means that together we all make up a group or a body of Christians.

The Bible goes on to say that each part is important. The eye can't say to the hand, "I don't need you." Or the head can't say to the feet, "I don't need you." So one Christian can't say to another, "You're not important to the church," or "You don't count." Each Christian is important to the body of Christ.

You too are important. Even though you're young, if you're a Christian, you're a member of the body of Christ. You're a body part, and God's given you a special job to do.

Maybe you're a mouth; then you can talk about God's love. Maybe you're a hand and are very good at helping people. Or an ear, to hear the call of those who need help. Or a foot, to bring God's Word to others. Each of you has a talent—some special way you can help the body of Christ.

Look around you at all these people in church. They're all different; they all have their own talents. But together, *we (Sweep your arm to include the children.)* make up the body of Christ. And you, as well as everyone else here, are an important member of that body.

6

Rooted in Christ

Scripture: So then, just as you received Christ Jesus as LORD, continue to live in him, rooted and built up in him, strengthened in the faith as you were taught, and overflowing with thankfulness (Col. 2:6, 7).

Theme: Just as a plant must have its roots in the ground to live and to grow well, so we must be firmly planted in Christ to grow as Christians.

Object: A potted plant with strong roots. Dig the plant up carefully so as not to disturb the roots; then replant it, solidly enough so it will stand straight, loosely enough, so that you can pull it up easily.

There's a text in the Bible that tells us to be rooted in Christ. Can anyone tell me what that means? What does rooted and built up mean? *(Pause for response.)* Maybe I can explain it. I brought this plant along to help all of us understand a little better.

This looks like a pretty healthy plant, doesn't it? It's growing straight and tall. It looks like it's getting enough food; it's doing fine.

Why do you think this plant is doing so well? Let me give you a hint. *(Remove the plant from the pot and shake some of the dirt off the roots.)* Will it keep growing now? *(Shake your head to elicit the right response.)* Then why was this plant doing so well? *(Pause for response.)* That's right,

17

it's healthy because it was growing in the dirt. It had its roots in the ground, where they belong.

These roots take tiny bits of food and water from the soil. That food and water travels from the roots to all parts of the plant. That's how the plant eats and drinks.

What happens when the roots are pulled from the ground? *(Pause for response.)* Yes, the plant will soon die. Roots can't pick food or water from the air. They must be planted firmly in the soil, so the plant can live.

When a plant has its roots firmly in the soil we say that the plant is well rooted. This plant was growing because it was well rooted.

That's what it means to be rooted in Christ. It means that you are planted firmly in him. You believe in Jesus Christ, and he's the most important thing in your life. You're like this plant, and Jesus is the solid earth that gives it life. Just like roots take in food and water, you listen to what Christ says in the Bible and use that to guide your life. And then you'll become a strong, healthy Christian, because you're rooted in Christ, depending on him.

7

Equal in Christ

Scripture: There is neither Jew nor Greek, slave nor free, male nor female, for you are all one in Christ Jesus (Gal. 3:28).

Theme: We are all equal in God's sight, through Christ.

Object: A picture of a group of animals that ranks itself into some social order (such as a pack of wolves, a flock of chickens, a band of monkeys, a herd of elephants). This lesson is done with a pack of wolves, but provisions are made for any social-ranking group.

Can you see this picture? It's a pack of wolves [flock of chickens, band of monkeys, or other]. They all look more or less the same, don't they? They're a bunch of animals grouped together.

But let me tell you something. If you were a wolf living in this pack, you wouldn't feel like you were the same as all the others.

You see, every pack of wolves has definite leaders. They tell the whole pack where to hunt, when to rest, and all sorts of things. They can even pick on other members of the pack if they want to. And if they don't like a certain wolf, they'll chase it out of the pack.

Then there are other wolves that aren't as important in the pack. They always try to please the leaders so that they can stay in the pack. Sometimes they're the ones that are picked on, and sometimes they pick on other wolves that aren't even as important as they are.

Some of these wolves are almost totally ignored. They live on the fringes of the pack. As long as they don't upset another wolf, they're allowed to stay—but they get picked on a lot.

You see, every [flock, band, or herd] of [whatever animal you have] has a definite leader [or two] that is the most important animal there. The leaders rule the [flock, band, or herd] and make the others do exactly what they want done. They can even chase one of the other animals out of the [flock, band, or herd] if they want to.

The rest of the animals aren't as important as the leaders, but they all have their place. Some are in the middle—sort of important, but not really. They try to please the leaders, but they also pick on some of the other animals. And some are way down at the bottom—not important at all—everybody can pick on them. They have to do whatever another animal wants them to do. They're just not important in the [flock, band, or herd].

It is interesting to know that chickens have a pecking order more than a leader-follower relationship. Top chicken can peck any other at will and gets first chance at the food. Lowest rank is pecked on by all and takes what it can get!

If you were a member of this pack, you would know exactly where you ranked. You would know which wolf was more important than you and which was less important.

We can't see that at all by looking at this picture, can we? To us, every wolf is equal; but the wolves don't think so.

In a way, we could say that people are sort of like these wolves. Some people tend to think that they're very important. They like to tell others what to do and have everybody follow them. They'll even ignore people who they think aren't as important as they are.

20

Others think they're kind of middle-of-the-pack, with some people more important and some less important than they. And then there are always people who feel as though they're on the very bottom; not worth much at all, not very important. Everybody seems to know exactly where he or she fits in, who's more important and who's less important than they.

Take a look at this picture again. You know what? God looks at us just like we look at this picture. We look at this and see wolves. God looks at us and sees his children. He doesn't see some that are very important and some that don't count at all. He sees us all as equals in Christ. No one counts any more than anyone else.

Sometimes you may feel that you don't count at all—that you're just a little kid and not worth very much. But remember that to God, you are just as important as anyone else.

8

Keep It Clean

Scripture: But now you must rid yourselves of all such things as these: anger, rage, malice, slander, and filthy language from your lips (Col. 3:8).

Finally, brothers, whatever is true, whatever is noble, whatever is right, whatever is pure, whatever is lovely, whatever is admirable—if anything is excellent or praiseworthy—think about such things (Phil. 4:8).

Objects: A clean transparent glass, a clean opaque glass (or a coffee mug), a pitcher of water, an empty bowl and a handful of dirt.

Theme: God wants us to be clean on the inside as well as the outside.

Everybody looks so fresh and clean today. I can tell that you probably washed and put on some nice, clean clothes before you came here.

Did you clean up inside as well as outside? God wants us to keep ourselves clean inside, you know. He's told us to get rid of *anger, rage, malice, slander,* and *filthy language* and think about whatever is *admirable* or *excellent* or *praiseworthy.*

That's a lot of big words. Let's see if I can make it clear.

Pretend that this glass is you *(Show them the clean,*

empty glass.), just the way you were born. As you grow, you begin to see things, hear things, and think about things. *(Pour some water into the glass.)* These are all thoughts going into your head. They're all good thoughts, the kind God wants you to think. *(Pour the glass about one-half full.)* Here you are, partly grown up, with good, clean thoughts inside of you.

This glass of water looks good doesn't it? We could drink it or clean with it. We could use it for several good things.

That's just like you—if you're clean inside. God can use you to do good things. You can speak kindly to people and show Jesus' love to those around you.

But here come some bad things. *(Drop clumps of dirt into the water as you list the bad things.)* You're angry at someone. You talk about a boy behind his back. You start thinking dirty thoughts. You use filthy language. You like to tell dirty jokes. Look what's happening to you inside. All that dirt is spreading around and ruining everything.

Would you use this glass of water? *(Pause.)* Of course not! You certainly wouldn't want to drink it, and it's too dirty to clean anything.

(Pour the dirty water into the opaque glass or cup. Leave some residue in the clear glass. Show them the opaque glass.) There, now at least you look clean on the outside. Is that any better? *(Pause for response.)* No, because you know that you're still dirty inside. You still can't use this water.

That's just like you, if you have dirty thoughts on the inside. Even if you look good to other people, God knows that you're dirty inside. And he knows he can't use you to do good things.

So he said that if you've got bad or dirty thoughts inside, get rid of them. *(Pour some clean water into the clear glass, swish it around to clean the glass, and empty it into the bowl.)* Fill yourself with good, clean thoughts. *(Pour some* more clean water into the glass.) If someone tries to put dirty thoughts into your head *(Take some dirt and hold it above the clear glass of water.)*, don't let them. *(Cover the glass and throw the dirt back into its container.)* Because God wants you to stay clean inside—for him.

9

Grow in Jesus

Scripture: "I am the vine; you are the branches. If a man remains in me and I in him, he will bear much fruit; apart from me you can do nothing" (John 15:5).

Theme: To be live Christians, we need Jesus.

Object: A healthy potted plant with branches. Break one branch from the plant and let it die. Put the dead branch in a bag.

I had a little accident with this plant. One of the branches broke off. The plant's okay, but the branch died. *(Take the dead branch out of the bag.)* It started to die as soon as it broke off the plant. I might as well throw this branch away. *(Put the branch on the floor behind you.)*

It's no surprise that the branch died, is it? After all, it has to be connected to the plant to live. How does this main stem help these branches live? *(Indicate stem and branches on the plant while pausing for responses.)* That's right. The stem sends food and water into the branches, so they can grow. The stem has little tubes that grow right into the branches. These little tubes carry everything that the branch needs to grow.

Can a branch live after it's broken from the plant? *(Shake your head to elicit the right response.)* Of course not. If it's broken off, the tubes are broken. Then the branch

25

can't get the things it needs to grow, and it will soon die.

Jesus once said that it's the same way with his people. He called us branches, and he called himself a vine. That's like the stem and branches of this plant. You can think of this stem as Jesus, and these branches as us. If we're connected to him, we can be strong healthy Christians. But if we're cut off from him, he said, we'll wither and die inside, just like this dead branch. You can't be a Christian without being connected to Jesus.

How can you be connected to Jesus? What can you do to make sure you're in touch with him? *(Pause.)* That's right. You can read your Bible and you can pray to him. Bible reading and prayer are the little "tubes" that help you grow as a Christian. Then he'll be the vine or the stem that helps you—the little branch—grow. He'll "feed" you everything you need through the "tubes" of the Bible and prayer.

What would happen if you broke those tubes? Could you be a good healthy Christian if you never prayed or paid any attention to the Bible? Of course not! Jesus said you would be like a broken branch that withers and dies. Just like that dead branch. We might as well pick it up and throw it away. *(Pick up the dead branch and put it back into the bag. Turn your attention back to the live plant.)*

These branches are much better. They look good, solid, and healthy, like good, healthy Christians.

What kind of a Christian do you want to be? A withered dead thing, like the branch in the bag, or a good, healthy one like these? *(Pause.)* Jesus wants you to be a solid healthy Christian, always connected to him.

10

Follow God

Scripture: Be imitators of God, therefore, as dearly loved children and live a life of love, just as Christ loved us . . . (Eph. 5:1, 2).

Trust in the LORD with all your heart and lean not on your own understanding; in all your ways acknowledge him, and he will make your paths straight (Prov. 3:5, 6).

The LORD delights in the way of the man whose steps he has made firm; though he stumble, he will not fall, for the LORD upholds him with his hand (Ps. 37:23, 24).

Theme: As followers of God, we should show love to all people. We should trust God to guide our lives, and he will not fail us.

Object: A picture of young ducks (geese, any waterfowl) following a parent.

Can you all see this picture? Someone tell me what it is. *(Pause for response.)* That's right, it's a bunch of young ducks following their mother. You've probably seen pictures like this before, or maybe you've even seen the real thing. Let me tell you a bit about this.

These little ducks are created to follow their mother automatically. Soon after they hatch, she leaves the nest, and they all follow her. She usually walks straight to

27

water, hops in, and swims away. All the little ones hop in without a fear and swim right behind her. Wherever she goes, they follow closely behind. They do exactly what she does. They never even think of doing anything different from that; they trust her completely.

The mother duck was created to automatically take good care of her young. She knows that they're following her. If she senses danger, she swims to a protected place, so her young will be safe. She won't swim out into open water until the danger is past, because she knows her young are following close behind. As long as her young follow her, she does all that she can to keep them safe.

Did you know that God wants us to be like these young ducks? He does. He wants us to follow him that closely. The Bible is full of calls to follow God.

Paul said that we should imitate God. Just as these little ducks do whatever their mother does, we should follow God so closely that we try to do what he does.

One big thing that God does is show his love to people. In fact, he loves us so much that he sent Jesus to die for us. So we should love people, too. If we follow God, others should be able to see it in the way we love people.

The Bible also says that we should trust in the Lord and not "lean on our own understanding." These little ducklings don't go off on their own. Instead, they trust in their mother to teach them where to go and what to do. That's the same way we should trust in God to show us how to live.

Remember I said that the mother duck was created to take good care of her young automatically? Well, even more certain than that is God's promise that he will take care of us. The Bible says that if we follow God, he will make our paths straight. He will show us how to live. And if we trust him as we follow him, he will not let us fall. He will help us whenever the going gets rough.

So in a way you can think of yourself as one of these little ducks. Trust in God and follow him. And he has promised to guide you.

11

Your Wonderful Body

Scripture: For you created my inmost being; you knit me together in my mother's womb. I praise you because I am fearfully and wonderfully made: (Ps. 139:13, 14).

Theme: Thank God for your wonderful bodies.

Objects: Nothing extra, only several children sitting on the floor in front of church.

Note: The time you have available should determine how many of these "experiments" you use.

I have nothing special with me today. Instead, I want you to use your imaginations and do a few experiments.

First, pretend that you have a very itchy nose. You want to scratch it, but you can't bend your arm. Try to scratch your nose once without bending your arm. *(Give the children a chance to try that.)* It's impossible, isn't it? You simply can't scratch your nose with your finger without bending your arm.

Imagine what life would be like if you had no elbows. Could you feed yourself? *(Shake your head and pause for responses.)* Could you comb your hair? Could you even throw a ball? Life would be rather tough if you had no elbows. Aren't you glad that God gave you elbows when he made you?

Now, pretend that there's a pretty, little flower on the floor in front of you. You want to pick it up and smell it, but you can't bend your fingers. Try to pick up the flower without bending your fingers. *(Give the children a chance to try that.)* That's almost impossible, too, isn't it? Maybe you can pick it up somehow with your thumb, but that would be very difficult.

Imagine what life would be like if you couldn't bend your fingers. Even if you had elbows, could you feed yourself? Could you pick up a crayon and draw a simple picture? Could you tie your shoelaces? Reach over, and try to hold the hand of the person next to you without bending your fingers. *(Pause.)* You can't even do that, can you? Aren't you glad God gave you fingers that bend?

Now try this. Look straight at me for fifteen seconds without blinking. It will be hard but try not to blink. I'll tell you when to start. *Go. (Time fifteen seconds.)* That was really impossible too, wasn't it? Your eyes probably started to hurt and to water when you didn't blink.

You usually blink about every 5 seconds, or 12 times a minute, or 720 times an hour. Blinking keeps your eyes moist and healthy. You don't have to think about it, because God made your eyes to blink automatically.

Imagine what would happen if you had to remind yourself to blink. You probably couldn't think of anything else. Even now as I am talking, I would say, "Blink. Aren't you glad . . . blink . . . that God made your eyes . . . blink . . . so that they blink by themselves? . . . blink!" And if you didn't remember to blink, your eyes would probably be ruined.

God gave you a wonderful body, with parts that work just right for what you have to do, and parts that work all by themselves, so you don't have to think about them. We don't think about that very often.

Long ago, King David thought about how well God had made his body. He even wrote it down in a psalm, so that we could be reminded once in a while. He said,

"I praise you (meaning God) because I am fearfully and wonderfully made."

"Fearfully made" doesn't mean that we're afraid. We never have to be afraid of our bodies. *Fearful* here means full of awe. Have you ever heard someone say, "That's awesome"? They usually mean something like, "That's just great." That's what David meant. In other words, he was saying, "Lord, God, you gave me a great, wonderful body."

Try to say that once. But—before you do—press your tongue down tightly against the bottom of your mouth. Don't move it. Now, try to say, "Lord, God, you gave me a great, wonderful body." *(Pause.)* You can't really talk without moving your tongue, can you? Aren't you glad God gave you a tongue that can move?

There are many wonderful things in our bodies that we never think about or take time to thank God for. Have you ever said, "Thank you, God, for my elbows, or my fingers, or my eyes"?

I said in the beginning that I had nothing special with me today, but I was wrong, wasn't I? I have my own wonderful body, and you have yours. Maybe this week we can remember to thank God for the bodies he's given us.

Before you go back to your seats, try one more experiment. Pretend that you don't have knees. Sit with your legs straight out in front of you. *(Pause.)* Now try to get up without bending your knees. *(Pause.)* Aren't you glad that God gave you knees?

Now you can go back to your seats. And on the way back, thank God for your wonderful body.

12

Bad Company; Good Friends

Scripture: Do not be misled: "Bad company corrupts good character" (1 Cor. 15:33).

Theme: Because we are influenced by those around us, we should choose our friends wisely.

Objects: Fruits which will mold easily. (Raspberries, strawberries, or oranges work well.) Purchase them well enough in advance of this lesson to let some of them go moldy. Bunch them together, so that the mold spreads among them. Keep some in the refrigerator (or purchase them later), so that they are still good. Put the moldy fruits in a glass bowl so that they can be easily seen. Put the good fruits in a paper sack.

There's something wrong with this fruit. *(Show them the moldy fruit in the bowl.)* What's the matter with it? *(Pause for response.)* That's right, its all moldy. I must have left it out too long. I don't think any of it's good. The mold must have spread from one raspberry [strawberry, orange] to another.

I do have some good raspberries [strawberries, oranges] here in this bag. Do you think I should put these in the bowl? *(Pause for response.)* No? Why not? *(Pause for response.)* I think you're right. If I put the good raspberries in with the bad, that mold would grow onto the good ones too. Then they would be bad. The good ones won't stay good if they're mixed with the bad. That's just the way it is.

That's the way it is with people, too. Good people often start doing bad things when they hang around with bad people. Sin has a way of spreading, just like the mold on this fruit. The Bible even warns us about that. It says that bad company corrupts good character.

Let me try to make that a little more clear. Let's say that you are very good at obeying your parents. You never think of talking back to them. But you know this person who isn't so good at that. He or she talks back to his (or her) parents and disobeys them quite often. You become friends with that person and spend a lot of time with him. First, you're shocked by the way he talks back to his parents. Pretty soon you become used to it because you hear it so much. And before you know it, you have to watch your tongue, or you're talking back to *your* parents too. What your friend has been doing affected you, sort of like this mold that grows from one fruit to another.

That's just a little example, but I think you get my point. Your friends do have an effect on you. That's why the Bible warns us about bad company.

God wants you to live a good life. He doesn't want you to be influenced by bad company. So when you choose your friends—people with whom you're going to spend a lot of time—think of that warning. Stay away from people who do bad things; you don't want that mold to grow on you, too. *(Show them the fruit in the bowl.)* Instead, choose people who do good things to be your friends. *(Hold up the bag.)* Then you won't have to worry about bad company.

13

God Will Supply

Scripture: . . . Open wide your mouth and I will fill it (Ps. 81:10).

And my God will meet all your needs according to his glorious riches in Christ Jesus (Phil. 4:19).

Theme: Trust in God to supply all your needs.

Object: A picture of baby birds, begging for food.

Can you all see this picture? Someone tell me what it is. *(Pause for response.)* That's right, it's baby birds, begging for food. You've probably all seen pictures like this before; maybe you've even seen the real thing. If you haven't let me tell you a little bit about this.

When these little birds first hatch, they're completely helpless. What they need most of all is food to make them strong. So they're created to naturally beg for food, like this. *(Open your mouth wide to mimic a young bird begging for food.)* They open their mouths as wide as they can, and completely trust their parents to bring them food.

The parent birds are created naturally to bring food to the little ones. They see those open beaks, and automatically they put food into the young birds' mouths. They do it again and again and again and again. Sometimes it seems like the little ones are never full. But the parents keep bringing food as long as the little birds keep begging for it.

Did you know that God wants you to act like a baby bird? He does. He said, "Open wide your mouth and I will fill it."

That doesn't mean that you're supposed to really open your mouth like this (Demonstrate.), and God will put food into it, does it? No. But it does mean that God will give you everything you need. He said it another way in the Bible when he had Paul write, "My God will meet all your needs. . . ."

In a way, we could say that God is like a parent bird. When the young ones beg for food, there's no doubt that the parent will feed them. When you ask, there's no doubt that God will give you everything you need, because he has promised that.

So we should be just like these baby birds. They completely trust their parents to bring them food. We should completely trust God to supply our needs.

Open wide your mouth, and trust God to give you everything you need.

14

Thank God for Little Things

Scripture: . . . "Sing and make music in your heart to the LORD, always giving thanks to God the Father for everything, in the name of our LORD Jesus Christ" (Eph. 5:19, 20).

Theme: We should thank God for all he has given us, even the little things.

Object: Raisins, enough so each child can have a few.

Note: The length of this lesson can be determined by the amount of time you have. Simply delete some discussion of "little things" for a shorter lesson.

I've brought a treat with me today. Raisins! You may each have a few, but please don't eat them yet. Just look at them for a little while. *(Pass out the raisins.)*

Raisins are funny-looking little things, aren't they? They're small and brown and all withered up. They really don't look like much.

But they're good. How many of you like to eat raisins? *(Pause.)* That's great, because raisins are good for you. They can help you stay healthy.

Where do raisins come from? *(Pause for reply. The answer will determine whether or not you skip the next paragraph.)*

That's right, raisins come from grapes. People pick

grapes and let them dry in the sun. As the grapes dry, they shrivel up and become raisins. But where do the grapes come from? *(Pause for reply.)*

Yes, they come from God. He made some grapes so that they could dry into these good raisins.

Did you ever thank God for raisins? Have you ever said, "Lord we thank you for this raisin"; "God is great, God is good, and we thank him for this raisin"?

That almost sounds a little silly, doesn't it? Yet the Bible says that we should thank God for everything. Raisins certainly are good little things that he gave us. Maybe we should thank him for them once in a while.

You know, God gives us lots of good little things, and often we forget to say *thanks*. Look around you for a minute. You can probably find several good, little things that God has given you.

Look out the window for a minute. *(This will work only if the children can see outside from where they are sitting. If not, get them started with a few of the paragraphs below.)* Can you see the sun shining? That's not really such a little thing. We need sunshine to make our food grow. But did you ever say, "Thank you, God, for sunshine"? *(or)* See all the clouds in the sky? Sometimes we don't like clouds, but we need them to bring rain. Did you ever say, "Thank you, God, for clouds"? Look at the grass. Animals need grass and other plants to eat. And grass holds the dirt in place. Did you ever say, "Thank you, God, for grass"?

(Now look around you right in the church.) I see lights. How could we see in here at night without lights? Of course people made those lights, but God gave people the ability to make them. Did you ever say, "Thank you, God, for lights"? I see places to sit. How would you like to come here and stand up straight and still for over an hour? Aren't you glad we have seats? Did you ever thank God for seats? What else do you see? *(Give the*

38

children a chance to respond. Enlarge a bit on each response, ending with "Did you ever thank God for _____?)

Now look at things closer to you. How about buttons [or zippers, or Velcro]? How could you get into your clothes without them? Or how could you keep your coat warm and snug around you without buttons? Again, they're just little things, and people made them. But God is really behind it all, directing those people, isn't he? Maybe we should thank God for buttons. What else do you see? *(Give the children another chance to respond and enlarge on it. This can go on as long as you want it to.)*

I think you get my point, don't you? God has given us many little, good things to enjoy. The Bible tells us to thank God for everything, but often we forget about the little things.

I didn't forget about your raisins. I know you're still holding them. I'd like you to try something with those raisins.

Take them back to your seat. You can even take them home. Let them remind you of all the good, little things that God has given you. If you want to eat one, think first of one good, little thing. Then say, "Thank you, God, for _____ [grass, lights, buttons, or something that's been mentioned] before you pop that raisin into your mouth. If you want to eat another one, think of another good thing, and thank God for that before you eat the raisin. That way you can remember to thank God for everything, even the little, good things.

15

Watch Your Tongue

Scripture: ". . . Consider what a great forest is set on fire by a small spark. The tongue also is a fire . . ." (James 3:5, 6).

Theme: Be careful that your words do not hurt others.

Object: A cigarette lighter, a book of matches, fireplace matches, or some other fire source—something which can burn for a few minutes is best.

(Light the lighter.) Look at this flame. It's really rather small, isn't it? And everything's okay if I'm very careful with it.

But if I begin to get careless, we could get into a lot of trouble here. Suppose I dropped this on the floor, or held it close to something flammable, what might happen? *(Demonstrate by holding the flame close to the flammable material, and pause for response.)* You're right; the carpet [or whatever you have close to the flame] might catch on fire. And when that starts burning, the benches [or something else nearby] might catch on fire, and maybe everything finally would burn.

That's why we're warned against playing with fire. One small flame like this can do a lot of damage if we're not careful. *(Blow out the lighter.)*

The Bible warns us about playing with another kind

of fire—our tongues. It says that the tongue is just like a small spark of fire; it too can do a lot of damage. You can get into a lot of trouble and hurt a lot of people with careless words.

It can work like this. Pretend you know someone named Harold *(Pick a name not represented there.)* One day you notice that he has a little spot on his ear. You say *(Light the lighter.)* to your best friend *(Put it near something flammable.)*, "Harold has dirt in his ear." Your friend says to someone else *(Indicate something nearby.)*, "Harold always has dirty ears. Gross." And *he* says to someone else, "Harold's always so gross and dirty. I'll bet he never takes a bath." And pretty soon everybody's thinking that poor Harold is the dirtiest kid in the neighborhood. All because of one small thing that you said *(Indicate the flame.)*.

Watch your tongue. *(Hold the flame up.)* It's just like a fire and can burn people. Think before you talk, and bite off those words that can hurt. *(Blow out the flame.)*

16

Live in God's Love

Scripture: "As the Father has loved me, so have I loved you. Now remain in my love. If you obey my commands, you will remain in my love . . ." (John 15:9, 10).

Theme: Just as plants need sunlight to grow, so we need God's love to grow spiritually.

Objects: Two potted plants. One should be healthy and the other dying or dead because it has been deprived of light. *(Take one and put it in a closet for a few weeks. Water it, but don't give it light.)*

Look at these two plants—how different they are. This one [the healthy plant] looks great, doesn't it? It usually sits by a window [or on the porch, or outside]. This one [the ailing plant] has been sitting in my closet for a few weeks. It doesn't look very healthy. In fact, I think it's dying [dead].

What makes the difference between these plants? *(Pause for response.)* That's right—sunlight! It's too dark in my closet. This plant [the ailing one] didn't get any light. This one [the healthy plant] is growing well because it lives in the sunlight. Plants need sunlight to live.

In a way, you're just like one of these plants. You don't especially need lots of sunlight to grow, although that's nice. You need something else to grow strong and

42

healthy inside. You need the warmth and light of God's love in your life.

If God didn't love you and surround you with that love, you'd be just like this sick plant. Inside, your heart and soul would be dead and lifeless, kind of dried up with no love. But God does love you and he pours that love around you like bright sunshine every day. You can soak up God's love and grow as a Christian, healthy and full of love inside.

But you're not exactly like these plants, are you? These plants have to try to grow wherever I put them. You can choose whether or not you're going to live in God's love. You can shut God out of your life, just like this plant was moved out of the sunshine; or you can open your heart and soul to God's love.

Long ago Jesus knew that you would have a choice. And he told you what he wants you to do. He said, "Remain in my love." He wants you to stay in that sunshine, to open yourself to his love.

How can you be sure that you stay in God's love? Jesus told you how. He said, "If you obey my commands, you will remain in my love." So what should you do? *(Pause for response.)* Yes, obey Jesus! And how do you know that you're doing what Jesus wants you to do? *(Pause.)* That's right! Read God's Word, the Bible—and pray. Then try to live how God wants you to live. Always stay close to God, and his love will help you grow.

So don't shut God out of your life and become like this sick, dried-up plant. Remain in the sunshine of his love, so you can grow strong and healthy as a Christian.

17

Secure in the Lord

Scripture: He who fears the LORD has a secure fortress, and for his children it will be a refuge (Prov. 14:26).

Theme: God protects those who trust in him.

Object: A hermit crab (available at most pet stores).

It looks like I have a shell here, but there's something living inside it. Can anybody guess what it is? (*Pause for response.*) It's a hermit crab!

The shell really isn't a part of the crab. When this little crab was born, it had no protection from its enemies. So it found an empty shell and crawled inside. The shell is like a little fort that the crab carries with it wherever it goes. When danger threatens—it thinks it's in danger now—it crawls into the shell, and then it's protected from its enemies.

There's one problem with this shell; it doesn't grow. The crab inside will grow, and someday the shell will be too small. Then the crab will have to find a bigger shell to use as its fort. It will quickly drop this old, smaller shell and scurry into the bigger one. Once inside, it will be safe again.

You'd almost think that this crab is quite smart, to find a shell for protection, wouldn't you? But we know that hermit crabs don't think about what they do; they just act on instinct. Who gave this crab the instinct to find a shell for protection? *(Pause for response.)* That's right, God did. God protects all of his creatures in some way.

God gave us a very special protection. The Bible says that anyone who fears the Lord has a secure fortress. That means that if you trust in God, he will protect you like a fort protects someone inside of it.

You could think of yourself as this little hermit crab. If you don't trust in God, it's as though you're crawling around without a shell. You can't always protect yourself from bad things that might happen. But when you put your trust in God, it's as though you're crawling into a shell. You have the protection of God's promise that he will always be with you.

There's one big difference between you and this hermit crab. Remember that I said this crab will grow, and soon the shell will be too small? Well, you can never outgrow God. He will always be big enough to protect you.

Put your trust in God, and he will always be there for you.

18

Signs of the Seasons

Scripture: As long as the earth endures, seedtime and harvest, cold and heat, summer and winter, day and night will never cease (Gen. 8:22).

Theme: The changing of the seasons is a sure sign that God keeps his promises.

Object: Spring: A sprig of blooming forsythia (or another plant taken as a sure sign of spring in your area).
Autumn: A few leaves which have changed color (or another sure sign of fall).

Note: This lesson is most effective in areas where seasonal changes are definite. It can be given at any change of season. Objects and illustrations used should be adjusted to fit your area. The lesson below can be used as a model.

Look what I found this week! *(Show them the forsythia.)* It's forsythia, one of the first things to bloom around here. This tells me that soon the grass will turn green, tulips will bloom, and leaves will unfold on the trees. Winter's about finished. This is a sure sign of spring.

What season will we have after spring? *(Pause for response.)* That's right, summer! The weather will turn hot; we'll be able to go swimming and have picnics outside. What comes after summer? *(Pause for response.)*

Sure, fall! The weather will get nippy, and we'll have to put on jackets again. And after fall comes . . . *(Pause for response.)* . . . yes, winter. We'll get out our mittens and boots, probably make a few snowmen and go ice skating. It will be cold enough to do those things; that's just the way winter is. But now winter is melting into spring and summer will follow. We can be absolutely sure of that.

Do you know why we're so absolutely sure that one season will follow another? *(Pause for response.)* It's because God promised. Long ago, he promised Noah that season would always follow season. And ever since that promise, we've had one season after another; spring follows winter and summer follows spring, just as he promised.

God never breaks his promises. He always keeps his word. When he promises something, you can be absolutely sure that he will do it.

God has given us many promises. Can you think of some? *(Pause for response.)* Let me help you. Didn't he promise that he would forgive our sins through Jesus? Didn't he promise that, if we prayed to him, he would answer us? Didn't he also promise that he would never leave us, that he would always be with us? The Bible is full of promises that God gave to us, and we know that he will keep every one of them.

That's why I'm so happy about this forsythia. I know it's a sure sign of spring. But, better than that, I know it's a sure sign that God keeps his promises.

So enjoy this new season. Go outside and do the things that you do in the spring. When summer comes, enjoy that too. As the seasons change, remember that God is keeping his promises to you. And he always will.

19

What's Inside Counts

Scripture: ". . . The LORD does not look at the things man looks at. Man looks at the outward appearance, but the LORD looks at the heart" (1 Sam. 16:7).

Theme: God looks at your heart, not your appearance.

Objects: A large glass jar and a big worm or several worms. Cover them with dirt and put the jar in a paper bag.

I have something very special with me today. *(Remove the jar from the bag very slowly to heighten suspense.)* It looks like it's only a jar of dirt, but there's something very special hidden in it. *(Shake the jar so that some of the worms show.)* A worm!

I can imagine that some of you are disappointed right now. You thought that you were going to see something very special, and all I have is a worm.

It doesn't look very special, does it? It's plain brown, and doesn't even seem to have a head. Its mouth is so tiny that you can't see it. It doesn't have any arms or legs. And it doesn't even make any noise; it just wiggles silently through the dirt. I can't see anything special about a common, little worm, can you?

But it *is* special; we just can't see what's so special about it. You have to know what's inside this worm to know what makes it special. You see, a worm eats dirt and other little things that it finds in the dirt. Somehow, inside of its body, all these things are mixed together to make a rich dirt. As the worm tunnels, it drops off this rich dirt. So, because of the way the insides of this worm were created, it helps make rich soil for our gardens.

Worms are very important in the ground. If we didn't have worms, we'd have a tough time growing any food.

Look at this worm once. It's so plain that you could never guess what a good, special thing it is by just looking at it. Its appearance, the way it looks, just doesn't mean much. It's what's inside that counts.

God tells us that the same thing is true about people; it's what's inside that counts. He said that people often look at outward appearances, but he looks at your heart.

You know what he means by "outward appearances," don't you? That's the clothes people wear, or how they comb their hair, or simply what they look like. Sometimes we even wish we were as good-looking as someone else, or had such nice clothes. Sometimes we're just not satisfied with the way we look. "If only I didn't have such mousy brown hair," you might say, or "If only I were taller."

But God says that none of those things matters. It's what's in your heart that counts. He wants you to have love in your heart, especially love for him. He looks straight through all those other things to what's inside you.

I think God would like us to look at people that way, too. What a person looks like shouldn't matter that much to us. If people are plain or good-looking, if they dress in the latest styles, or in old clothes, shouldn't make a difference. Often the plainest people can be our truest friends, with hearts of gold.

But most of all, you should remember that God

doesn't care at all what you look like or what you wear. You could be plain as this little worm—although no one is—and still God would love you. Because he looks at your heart.

20

Living Water

Scripture: "Whoever drinks the water I give him will never thirst. Indeed, the water I give him will become in him a spring of water welling up to eternal life" (John 4:14).

Theme: Just as all life depends on water, so our eternal life depends on Jesus, the Living Water.

Objects: Two live flowers. Pick them at least twenty-four hours before you use them. Put the stem of one in water and leave the other dry.

I picked these flowers about a day ago. *(Show the dry flower and the one in clear water.)* One seems to be doing much better than the other. What makes the difference? *(Pause for response.)* Of course, I put one in water! It will be able to live much longer than this dry flower.

Water is absolutely necessary for life. Without it, we all die; that's why this flower [the dry one] is starting to die.

Jesus knew how important water is to us. That's why he called himself *The Living Water*. He said that whoever drinks his water will never be thirsty again. And that water, he said, will become a spring of eternal life.

Now Jesus doesn't come and offer us each a glass of

magic water, does he? He didn't mean that we would never have to drink water again.

He was talking about something much more important than our bodies. What do you think he was talking about? *(Pause for response.)* That's right, he was talking about our souls!

When Jesus said he was Living Water, he meant that only he could keep our souls alive. The water he gives us isn't the water we see here. The water he gives us is forgiveness of our sins. When we say, "I believe that Jesus died for my sins," we're drinking *his* living water.

Without Jesus' living water, without the belief that he died for our sins, we can't live forever with him. Our souls will become like this flower [the dry one], because they don't have living water.

But when we do believe in Jesus, when we drink his living water, our souls can stay like this [the flower in water], alive with him forever.

So drink deeply of Jesus' living water. Believe in him, pray to him, read what he tells you in the Bible. Then your soul will never die like this [the dry flower]. Instead, you'll be alive [the live flower], like this—forever.

21

It All Belongs to God

Scripture: The earth is the LORD's, and everything in it, the world, and all who live in it (Psalm 24:1).

Theme: All of creation belongs to God; take care how you treat it.

Objects: A daisy or some flower with several petals; a spider in a jar.

I picked this flower early this morning [or whenever]. I wanted to show you what we used to do with flowers like this. Maybe you've done it too.

He/she loves me, he/she loves me not, he/she loves me, he/she loves me not. *(Pick off the petals as you say this.)* Have you ever done that? It's just a silly little custom; it doesn't really mean anything. This flower can't tell me if someone loves me or not.

If I wanted to do it again, I'd have to pick another flower, wouldn't I? This one isn't good anymore. I might as well throw it away.

While I was out getting the flower, I found this spider, so I brought it in to show you. *(Show spider in the jar.)* It doesn't look like it's very happy in the jar; perhaps I ought to let it go. *(Shake the spider onto the floor some distance from the children. Wait for a reaction.)*

What's the matter? Don't you like the spider? It's

more afraid of you than you are of it. It's probably just looking for a nice juicy bug to catch. What shall I do with it now that it's out? Get rid of it? Step on it? That's our first reaction when we see a spider inside, isn't it? Get rid of the thing. But I think I'll just put it back in the jar, so I can let it go later. *(Put the spider back in the jar.)*

You see, spiders have a very important place in creation. They help keep the bug population in check. If we didn't have spiders, we'd have 'way too many bugs. This is just one spider, but there's no sense in killing it. God made it for a purpose, so maybe we should let it live.

Besides that, whose spider is this? *(Pause.)* That's right, it's God's. God gave it life; we shouldn't kill it for no good reason. God made it and even though it's just a tiny thing, it belongs to him.

The Bible says that the earth and everything in it is God's. The world and everything that lives in it belongs to him. That certainly includes this spider. It included that flower, too, but the flower's no good anymore. I ruined it.

Do you think God is pleased when we ruin little bits of his creation like that? *(Pause.)* Of course not! How would you feel if someone took a pretty picture that you drew and tore it apart? Not very good, right?

In a way, being careless with creation is the same thing. We're taking something from God, a bit of his creation, and ruining it. He took a lot of care to create it well and make it all fit together. He even put us in charge of it, but not to ruin it. It still belongs to him, and we should be very careful with it.

So when you see a flower or a spider or any little thing, remember that the earth and everything in it is God's. We can enjoy it, but certainly not destroy it. Be careful how you treat God's creation.

Now, would someone like to take this spider outside and let it go?

22

Called by Name

Scripture: ". . . He calls his own sheep by name . . ." (John 10:3).

". . . Before I was born the LORD called me; from my birth he has made mention of my name" (Isa. 49:11).

Theme: God knows us intimately and calls us each by name.

Objects: A glass jar containing many ants (flies, gnats, or even worms; any living creatures that you can collect in abundance).

Note: You should know at least some of the children's names and a few details about them to make this effective.

I've brought some strange "pets" with me today—ants [flies, worms]! I've been watching them for a while now, and am getting to know them just a little bit. In fact, I've begun to name them.

There's Esmerelda. *(Point out one ant.)* She's the busiest one of the bunch. She looks like she's working all the time, even in this jar. There's Alexandra. *(Point out another one.)* She wants to get out more than any other ant in there. This is Horatio. He's always sleepy. And here's Percival. He looks a little confused. *(And so forth. Try to use names that none of the children have.)*

Let me pass the jar around so that you can have a

good look at these ants. *(Pass the jar around.)* Can you tell the difference between Esmerelda, Alexandra, Horatio, and Percival? *(Pause for response.)*

I'll tell you a secret; I can't tell the difference either. There are so many ants in there, I couldn't possibly name them all or keep them all separate. I was just kidding about getting to know them. They all look the same to me.

Some people think that's what we look like to God—a bunch of ants. After all, God is so big and so great, they say, we must look like nothing but tiny ants to him. And there are so many people in the world—billions of us—and he's so busy, he probably doesn't take any notice of us at all. If he does, we probably all look the same to him, just like these ants look all the same to us.

Do you think that's the way God looks at us, as if we're a bunch of ants? *(Pause for response.)* No, not at all! God knows each one of us by name! He is so interested in you and loves you so much that he knows you even better than you know yourself.

God can look at us right now and say, "There's Shelly. She's such a thoughtful person. There's David. He's going to his grandmother's tomorrow. There's Lisa. She's one of my happy children." *(Continue with as many children as you can name.)*

I probably can't even name all of you here, and I don't know some of you as well as I would like to. But God does. He calls each of you by name and watches over you with love every minute of every day.

I'll take my jar of ants back now, and let them go after the service. Next time you see an ant, it may be Esmerelda, Alexandra, Horatio or Percival. You'll never know for sure.

But one thing you can know for sure; you are never this little *(Direct attention to the ants.)* in God's eyes. You are one of his children; he knows you by name and loves you.

23

God Sees All

Scripture: Nothing in all creation is hidden from God's sight. Everything is uncovered and laid bare before the eyes of him to whom we must give account (Heb. 4:13).

Theme: God sees all that we do.

Objects: A dead, brownish moth (or any small insect which blends with its surroundings) in a jar with dead leaves and twigs (or any natural objects with which it blends); a clean sheet of white paper.

Can you find the moth in this jar? It's rather difficult, isn't it? That's because the moth blends so well with its surroundings. It's dead now, but even when it's alive, it can hide very easily. It sits perfectly still in litter like this, and it's almost impossible to find.

Maybe this will help you see it. *(Pull the moth out of the jar and hold it up in front of the white paper.)* There—now it isn't hidden; you can see it perfectly well.

Have you ever tried to act like a moth? That sounds silly, doesn't it? Yet I think that most of us have tried to act like a moth sometime or other.

Let's say that Mom or Dad told you not to eat any more cookies before dinner, but you wanted one so much. So very quietly you tiptoed over to the cookie jar, carefully lifted the lid, and took one cookie. Then you tiptoed to your bedroom and quietly ate the cookie. You got away with it because no one noticed you. You were acting like a moth.

(You may want to substitute something from your own experience for the following paragraph. The idea is to let the children know that everyone—not just children—has something they would like to hide.)

I remember acting like a moth once. I was at school, playing with a bunch of other kids in a place we were not supposed to play. The principal caught us and made us all come and stand in front of him. So I stood right in the very middle of the group, hunched myself down a little and stayed very still, hoping he wouldn't notice me. I was trying to act like a moth, hide myself so he wouldn't notice. *(Drop the moth back into the jar at this point.)*

Sometimes people think they can get away with acting like a moth. They do something wrong and keep very quiet about it. They think they're okay because no one has noticed.

But Someone *has* noticed. The Bible says that nothing in creation is hidden from God's sight. Everything is laid bare before him. Although we can hide things that we do from people, God sees those things this clearly. *(Take the moth and put it in front of the paper again.)* Nothing that we do is hidden from him. He can see everything.

So the next time you want to sneak that cookie, or do something just a little bit wrong, remember this [the moth in front of the paper]. God sees everything that you do, even if no one else does.

But you can also remember that God loves you. He's not only watching you all the time, he's also always watching *over* you.

24

Be Yourself

Scripture: Each one should test his own actions. Then he can take pride in himself, without comparing himself to somebody else, for each one should carry his own load (Gal. 6:4, 5).

Theme: We should not compare ourselves to others, but develop our own God-given talents.

Object: A bouquet of several different flowers. Put them in a vase or jar in front of church, where people can see them.

Note: The length of this lesson can be determined by the variety of flowers you pick. Suggestions for many are given below.

I brought a bouquet of all different types of flowers to church today. I've been looking at this bouquet, trying to figure out which flower is the best of the lot. Maybe you can help me. Which one do you like best? Why? *(Pause for response and comment on each one, listing a strong point and how it differs from the others. See suggestions below.)*

The rose is pretty, and it smells so sweet, but it doesn't last very long. The dandelion doesn't smell as nice as the rose, but it's much more hardy. Dandelions can bloom almost anywhere. This iris, in a way is prettier than a common dandelion, but it won't grow in a

59

shady place. Some people don't like this milkweed at all, but I think the flower is unique. If you look at it closely, it's really very beautiful. And milkweed plants are very useful. The blue on this chickory is so cheerful, maybe this is the best one. But then, the daisies are nice, too; and they don't close up at night the way chickory does. Did you notice these tiny white flowers? Some people don't even see them, but they make a very good ground cover. They help hold dirt in place, even when it rains really hard. And this green one that doesn't look like much at all is a grass flower. Almost nobody would pick that as the best one, yet it holds seeds to make more grass. And grass is one of the most important plants in the world. Lots of animals eat grasses. We even eat some kinds of grasses.

I give up. I don't think we can say that any one of these flowers is better or more important than the rest. Each one is good in its own way.

Suppose these flowers could talk. Do you think they'd like what they are? The dandelion might say, "I want to be a rose." But then it couldn't live any place it wanted to. Or the milkweed might say, "I want people to admire me the way they admire that iris." But then it wouldn't be such a useful plant. The grass might say, "I'm tired of being such a funny little flower. I want to be a daisy." But then, what would the animals eat? They don't often chew on daisies. Maybe it's good that these flowers can't think or talk, or compare themselves to other flowers. Now they grow just as they were created to grow, each one for its own purpose. And, put together, they really make a very pretty bouquet.

I see another bouquet in church today—you! When I look at all of you together, I see a whole bouquet of beautiful little people, blooming for God.

You are a lot like this bouquet of flowers, aren't you? Each of you is different from every other person here. Each of you has your own special talents that God has given you.

If someone asked me to pick out the best person from among you, I couldn't possibly do it, could I? Just like the flowers, you're all different from each other, and you all have your good points.

Did you ever look at someone else and wish you were just like them? Maybe you felt like a dandelion comparing yourself to a rose. We all do that at times. We compare ourselves with someone else, and then we forget about our own good points.

God knew we would do that once in a while. That's why he said, "Each one should test his own actions. Then he can take pride in himself, without comparing himself to somebody else. . . ."

God wants you to develop the talents that he's given you, without comparing yourself to someone else. You are special in your own way, and that's the way God wants you to develop. When you don't compare yourself with anyone else, but just work to be the best you can be, you become a very special flower for God.

And then, if we all work together with our own talents, we become a beautiful bouquet for God.

25

Let's Pull Together

Scripture: Each of you should look not only to your own
interests, but also to the interests of others (Phil. 2:4).

Carry each other's burdens, and in this way you will
fulfill the law of Christ (Gal. 6:2).

Theme: We should help one another.

Objects: Live ants in a glass jar, a dead insect (a grasshopper would be excellent) in another jar.

Can you see what I have in this jar? *(Show
them the jar of ants and pause for response.)* That's right, live
ants walking all over the place. They're probably looking for a way to get out, or maybe they're looking for
some food. They haven't eaten since I caught them.

What do I have in this jar? *(Show them the jar with the
dead insect and pause for response.)* Yes, a dead bug [grass-
hopper]. Some kinds of ants like to eat dead bugs
[grasshoppers].

What would happen if put this dead bug [grass-
hopper] on the ground and then released the ants right
next to it? *(Pause for response.)* You're right! If these ants
are the kind that like to eat dead bugs, they would
swarm all over this grasshopper. Would they eat it right
away? *(Pause for response.)* Probably not. They'd probably try to drag it back to their home and eat it there.

You've seen that happen, haven't you? A bunch of ants work together to drag some big piece of food back to their home. Sometimes you see them pushing and pulling on a dead bug; sometimes they're working on a piece of food you may have left in the wrong place. But they're not eating it; they're trying to get it home so that all the ants can eat. And the ones that have found it work together to drag it home.

You see, ants live together in an ant city. Different ants in that city have different jobs. The ants that we see are workers that have gone out for food. Sometimes they'll eat a little while they're out, but they'll always carry some food home, too. They seem to know that there are other hungry ants back at the ant city.

And if one ant finds something that's too big for it to carry, it goes back to the ant city for help. More workers come out, so that they can drag the thing together, and help feed the whole ant city. It really is amazing the way these ants work together and help each other.

But then, maybe that shouldn't be so amazing. Maybe we should be used to workers helping one another.

In a way, we could say that we're like an ant city. We all have different interests and different things to do. But we all know each other and live fairly close to one another. And most important, we're all Christians [we all belong to this church], and that makes us all part of one big group. So we should all be working together.

The Bible tells us that we should look after the interests of others and carry each other's burdens. That means that if someone needs help, we should automatically offer help. We shouldn't think only of ourselves. We should do what we can for others and to help others in their work.

Then, just like these ants pulling on this grasshopper, we can pull together to do God's work in this world.

26

Consider the Dandelions

Scripture: "If that is how God clothes the grass of the field, which is here today, and tomorrow is thrown into the fire, how much more will he clothe you, O you of little faith!" (Luke 12:28).

Theme: God supplies our needs.

Object: A dandelion plant, roots and all, and one dandelion gone to seed, if you can find it. (It would be ideal, but not necessary, to have one dandelion flower for each child.)

You all know what this is, don't you? *(Show them the dandelion and pause for response.)* That's right, it's a dandelion plant. People don't think much of dandelions, but I think God gave it special attention when he created it.

See these leaves? *(Point out the various features as you mention them.)* They each have a little channel in the middle that helps water run straight down toward the plant. This root [the taproot] is so tough, you can hardly pull it from the ground. If you just pick the top of the plant and leave the root, it will grow a whole new plant! The flower stems are rather floppy so that they bend in the wind; they won't break. And the flowers themselves are like tiny miracles. *(Pass out the flowers if you have them.)*

This whole blossom will close to protect itself when it gets dark or when it rains. And then it will open again when the sun shines. Look at this blossom closely. Each of these yellow "petals" is really a whole tiny flower. Its parts are too small for us to see, so it looks like one petal. Each of these "petals" can make a whole new dandelion seed. And when the seed is ready, it has its own little parachute, so the wind can blow it away. *(Show the blossom gone to seed if you have it.)* You've all seen dandelion parachutes [or puff balls], haven't you? Sometimes, we'll blow on them and watch the seeds scatter. *(Demonstrate.)* Else a wind will blow them away, so they can make new dandelion plants.

I think God gave this plant exactly what it needs to grow well, don't you? *(Pause for response.)* This is only one little plant that he cares for. Does this tell you something about the way he'll care for you?

You mean much more to God than a dandelion plant. After all, you're his child. If God put this much care into one little plant, do you think he'll forget you? *(Pause for response.)* Of course not! He's promised to always take care of you.

Jesus said that we should look at flowers in the field, see how God takes care of them, and remember that he will always care for us. That's a promise.

So when you see dandelions growing outside [or when you look at this flower I gave you] you can think about how God cares for them. And that can remind you that he will always care for you.

27

Stop Your Picking;
Live in Love

Scripture: The entire law is summed up in a single command: "Love your neighbor as yourself." If you keep on biting and devouring each other, watch out or you will be destroyed by each other (Gal. 5:14, 15).

Theme: Picking at one another only destroys all involved; Christians should concentrate on loving one another.

Objects: A wasp and a spider in a jar together. You can use any combination of two creatures, each of which are adequately armed and which don't get along (such as two different spiders, a wasp and a hornet, a bee and a wasp, and so forth). The outcome of their imprisonment together in a jar is unpredictable, and you will have to adjust the lesson accordingly.

Can you see what I have in this jar? It's two creatures which should never be put together: a wasp and a spider. They usually don't live together, and when you put them in a jar like this, you can never tell what's going to happen.

What could happen in this jar? *(Pause for response.)* Yes, the spider could bite the wasp. [I think it already has.] Or the wasp could sting the spider. [I think it already has.] [Or both.] Sometimes they'll fight so much that they both kill each other. [I think they already have.] They could go to their own corners of the jar and live in an uneasy peace. But that usually doesn't happen, because they don't think these things out. They just fight it out and often destroy each other.

It's not a good idea to put a spider and a wasp together, because they're not meant to live together. I did this just to make a point.

Sometimes we can be an awfully lot like spiders or wasps, can't we? If there's someone we don't like very much, we want to bite at them a little with words. Or we'd like to sting them with something we say. We tend to pick a little at people we don't like.

Sometimes they'll pick back, and bite at you and sting you with words. Then you get a fight going, and just like this spider and wasp, you start to destroy each other.

That's not good, is it? The Bible even warns us about that. God said, "If you keep on biting and devouring— that's like eating—each other, watch out or you will be destroyed by each other."

What are you supposed to do, if there's someone you can't get along with? Should you ignore each other, like spiders and wasps usually do? Sometimes you can't. Then should you fight it out? *(Pause for response.)* No, God told us not to do that.

God also told us what we should do. He said that we should love our neighbors as ourselves. Would you pick on yourself or fight with yourself? Would you say something nasty about yourself to someone else, or make some stinging remark about yourself? *(Pause for response.)* Of course not. Then you shouldn't do that about someone else either. You should love every one and treat each person as you want to be treated. Then you won't destroy someone else and yourself by picking.

It may be very difficult to love some people, but God can help you. If you ask him, he can put the love of Jesus in your heart. Then you can be kind to people, rather than picking on them.

Spiders and wasps were never meant to live together, and they probably will always destroy each other when put together. But we're not spiders and wasps, although we act like it sometimes. We're *people*—God's special creatures. And he told us not to fight but to love each other instead.

28

Just Testing

Scripture: Test everything. Hold on to the good. Avoid every kind of evil (1 Thess. 5:21, 22).

Theme: We should constantly test new things (friends, ideas, actions) to avoid the bad and hold onto the good.

Object: A daddy longlegs in a jar.

Can you see what I have in this jar? It's not really a spider; it has a special name. What is it? *(Pause for response.)* It's a daddy longlegs. You've all seen daddy longlegs, haven't you?

There's something special about the way daddy longlegs walks. I can't show you here. But the next time you see a daddy longlegs outside, watch it very closely.

You see, daddy longlegs has eyes on top of its body, and it looks up rather than forward. It can't see where it's going. So it usually walks quite slowly.

But God gave it special testing legs. If you would look closely at this daddy longlegs *(You might want to pass the jar around.)*, you can see that one pair of legs in the front is longer than all the others. These legs are very sensitive; they help daddy longlegs feel, smell, and taste everything around it.

When daddy longlegs walks, it puts out this pair of legs first. It tests everything nearby with these legs. If it touches something that is not good for it, it avoids that thing. If it touches something that it knows is good, like good food or a sturdy place to walk, it will hang onto that good thing. *(You may want to demonstrate while you are talking. Look up at the ceiling, walk slowly while moving your arms in front and to your sides, testing things nearby with your hands.)* Watch daddy longlegs walk sometime, and you'll see it testing everything with those special legs.

And as you watch, you can think that that's the way God wants you to test things. God tells us to test everything, to hold onto the good and avoid bad things.

God gave us special testers, too, didn't he? *(Point to your head.)* That's right, he gave us brains, and he wants us to use them to test things.

We can test people. Think a minute about one of your friends. Is it someone who helps you do good things? Good! Or is it someone who gets you into trouble? Avoid troublemakers; make friends with good people.

We can test actions. A playmate says to you, "Let's go to the highway [some busy street near you] and throw stones at cars." Think a minute. Is that a good or a bad thing to do? *(Pause for response.)* Avoid doing bad things.

We can even test ideas. I'll give you two. We should love people. We should hate people. Think a minute about which idea is best. Should we hate people? *(Pause for response.)* No! Should we love people? *(Pause for response.)* Yes! Now you tested two ideas. You threw out the bad one and held onto the good one.

That's what God wants us to do in all things. Keep testing, testing, *testing*. Hold onto what is good. Avoid whatever is bad. Just like daddy longlegs tests everything it touches, so we should test everything that touches our lives.

29

Who Made You?

Scripture: Remember your Creator in the days of your youth . . ." (Eccles. 12:1).

Theme: God made us, and we are his.

Objects: A potted plant, an insect in a jar.

Note: Depending on your time, you may want to use one or both of these. Suggestions for both are given below.

This looks like a rather simple plant doesn't it? *(Show them the plant and point out various features as you are talking.)* Actually, it's very complicated. These leaves take sunshine and turn it into food. That's something we can't do; only a plant can do that. The roots, down where you can't see them, take water out of the ground. Even if the ground is just a little damp, somehow the roots manage to get water from it. And these stems aren't just sticks to hold the plant up. Inside each stem dozens of tiny tubes carry water one way and food another way, and everything that the plant needs to live right to the place where it's needed. Any plant really is a wonderful, complicated, living thing.

Some people say that plants just happened; they just started to grow all by themselves. Do you think a plant like this can just happen, without anyone making it?

(Shake your head and pause for response.) Of course not; someone had to make this plant.

Do you think any person could ever make a living plant? Could we paste leaves, roots, and stems together and make a plant grow? *(Pause for response.)* Of course not! No person can make a plant.

Then, who made this plant? Who caused it to grow so perfectly? *(Pause for response.)* Of course. God did. God made all plants.

Now let's look at something more complicated yet—a bug. *(Show them the insect and point out various features while you are talking.)* This thing walks on six legs, and never gets those legs mixed up. [It can fly, and no one taught it how.] And that hair [or, it has tiny hairs that we can't even see] on its body isn't just hair. It's like a lot of tiny weather instruments that tell the bug how hot or cold it is, how fast the wind's blowing, and if it's wet or dry outside. Inside its body, this bug has a tiny heart, a stomach, even a brain. Some people don't like bugs, but bugs really are wonderful little, living creatures.

Some people think that bugs just happened—that they just started to live all by themselves. Do you think bugs just happened, or did someone make them? *(Pause for response.)* Of course! A bug can't just happen; someone had to make them.

Can any person make a bug? Can we glue legs and feelers and wings together and make a living bug? *(Pause for response.)* Of course not! No person can make a bug.

Then who made this bug? Who gave it a tiny heart and stomach and brain? *(Pause for response.)* Of course, God did. God made all living creatures.

Now let's go to the most complicated creature of all—you! Look at your hand for a minute. Make a fist and move your fingers back and forth. *(Demonstrate.)* Everything works perfectly, doesn't it? Put your hand on top of your heart. *(Demonstrate.)* Can you feel it beat? It does that without your ever telling it to, just to keep you alive. And your brain is much more amazing than any computer. Think of all the things you are hearing and seeing and smelling right now. *(Pause.)* Your brain sorts out all those things and lets you think about what I'm saying. Besides all that, you have a soul, that part of you that's really you and will never die. You are—by far—the most complicated and wonderful creature on earth.

Yet, some people say that you just happened, too. They say that people weren't created by anyone; people just started to live. Can you believe that? Do you think people just happened? *(Pause for response.)* Of course not! Someone had to create us.

Can a person create another person? Can we sew a hand, a heart, and a brain together and give it life and a soul? *(Pause for response.)* Of course not!

Then, who created you? Who gave you life and a soul? *(Pause for response.)* Of course. God did!

You knew that all along, didn't you? You've probably learned since you were a baby that God made you. That's nothing new to you.

Yet the Bible tells us to remember our Creator. So it's good to repeat things like this: *God made you.* Don't let anyone tell you that he didn't. Always remember that God is your Creator.

You can see many wonderful things that God created all around you, but none is as wonderful as you are. Yet the things that you see can help you to remember that God created you, and you are his forever.

30

True to Your Label

Scripture: "You shall not misuse the name of the LORD your God . . ." (Exod. 20:6).

Theme: Christians should always try to act Christ-like. Failure to do so is misusing God's name.

Objects: Two opaque containers (margarine tubs) with lids. A label, HOUSEFLY, on one container and a label, HORNET, on the other.

What do you think is in this container? *(Hold up the HOUSEFLY container so that they can read the label and pause for response.)* That's right, a *housefly*. How do you know? *(Pause for response.)* Yes, that's what the label says. What do you think is in this container? *(Hold up the other container so that they can read the label and pause for response.)* Right, a *hornet*. At least that's what the label says.

Would you mind very much if I opened this container [the HOUSEFLY tub] and let whatever is in here fly free? *(Pause and shake your head to elicit the right response.)* Probably not. The label says it's only a fly. Would you mind if I opened this container? *(Show them the HORNET tub; pause and nod your head.)* Probably, right? Because there's supposed to be a hornet in here, and it may be angry at being caught. No one wants an angry hornet nearby.

What if I opened this container [the HOUSEFLY tub], and an angry hornet flew out? I think you'd be rather surprised and probably angry at me. After all, the label said that it was a housefly, and that's what you expect. The label would be a lie.

It's important for a label to be correct; what's inside should match the label. If not, you can't trust the label, and that's not good.

That's how it is with us too. We have one very important label that should be absolutely correct. That's the label CHRISTIAN.

Who can tell me what the word *Christian* means? *(Pause for response.)* That's right; it means we believe in Jesus [or whatever the response was], we are followers of Christ. We are labeled with Christ's name.

If we say we're Christians, if we carry Christ's label, then what's inside of us should be like Christ.

What should we have inside of us, to be like Christ? Should we have love or hate? *(Pause for response.)* What else should we have? *(Pause for response. If no responses are forthcoming, make suggestions like, joy, peace, helpfulness, wanting to do God's will, obeying God, and so forth.)* That's right, and what we have inside of us should be obvious to everyone.

If we are Christians, we should try to be like Christ. We should show our love and joy and helpfulness to others. After all, our label CHRISTIAN uses Christ's name to tell everyone who we follow.

If we are not like Christ, our label is a lie, isn't it? Then we're using Christ's name to fool others. We're using his name in the wrong way, and God told us never to misuse his name.

How many of you call yourself a *Christian*? *(Raise your hand so that the children will follow suit.)* That's wonderful. Never forget that you carry Christ's name. Always try to be true to your label: CHRISTIAN.

31

Watch What You Say About Others

Scripture: Do not let any unwholesome talk come out of your mouths, but only what is helpful for building others up according to their needs, that it may benefit those who listen. Be kind and compassionate to one another, forgiving each other, just as in Christ God forgave you (Eph. 4:29, 32).

Theme: Always try to say good about others. Never tear them apart with your words.

Object: Two flowers, each with several petals. Wrap a wet cloth around the stems to keep them fresh.

We're going to pretend for a little while. Who would like to help me? *(Pause.)* __[name]__ [a child who volunteered], will you come up and stand right beside me? You can hold this flower. Hold it up nice and straight.

We're going to pretend that this flower is _____ [the child who volunteered]. It's nice and straight and tall, a beautiful flower, just the way God made it. _____ is a beautiful person, just the way God made him/her. So we'll call him/her one of God's little flowers.

Now, remember, this is just pretend. We're going to say something mean about _____. Maybe, "_____ is a sissy." *(Done in a sing-song voice. You may want to move close to the child and put your arm around him/her as a little protection from the verbal onslaught.)* Or "_____ is a dummy."

How do you think that will make _____ feel? Probably like this. *(Tear a few petals from the flower.)* Every time you say something mean about _____, he/she feels like you're tearing him/her apart.

You like _____, but pretend you're angry at him/her for some reason. So you say, "I'm never going to play with you again." *(Tear off more of the flower.)* Or, "You're not my friend." *(Finish tearing the flower apart.)*

And how does _____ feel? Almost like this flower, all torn apart—as though it's not worth much at all.

Now let's try to put this flower back together again, *(Pick up some petals and try to attach them to the flower stalk.)* It doesn't work very well, does it? Let's try a little harder. *(Pick up some more petals and try to attach them to the flower stalk as you speak.)* It still doesn't work. This flower simply can't be put together again.

That's probably how _____ feels inside. She/he heard what we said. Even if we didn't mean it, the damage is done. We've made _____ feel awful inside, at least for a while, and we can't change that.

So, let's start over. *(Take out the other flower and give it to the volunteer. Help him/her hold it at about waist level.)* Here's _____, one of God's little flowers. He/she's a little shy, so he/she's not letting you know exactly how he/she feels inside.

Let's see if we can make that flower bloom nice and tall. I'll start. _____, you have such a lovely smile *(Or anything nice you can think to say about the volunteer. As you say it, help the child raise the flower just a little bit.)* Who would like to add to that? Think of something nice to say to _____. *(As the children say nice things, help the volunteer raise the flower. Add some things yourself. Try to make sure more good things are said than were bad things said at first. At the end, the child should be holding the flower straight up.)* Now we have a beautiful flower, and we helped it bloom straight and tall by what we said. That's much better, isn't it?

God talked about this very thing in the Bible. He knew that sometimes we would say things that are not nice about each other. So he told us to say only things that are helpful to others, to build them up. He said that we should be kind to each other. That way we can help them bloom.

So when you're tempted to say something mean or not very nice about someone, think of this flower. *(Show the ruined flower.)* Try not to tear anyone apart inside. Instead, say good, helpful things. *(Hold up the good flower.)* Then we can all help each other bloom.

32

Butterflies for Jesus

Scripture: But now you must rid yourselves of all such things as these since you have taken off your old self with its practices and have put on the new self, which is being renewed in knowledge in the image of its Creator (Col. 3:8–10).

Theme: Just as a caterpillar completely changes in a cocoon, so we should change our natures in Christ.

Objects: A caterpillar in a jar with a few leaves and a stick (and a butterfly if you can get one.)

I found this caterpillar on the ground a few days ago. It was probably making its way toward some plant to munch on a few leaves. So I picked it up to show it to you.

A caterpillar doesn't lead a very nice life, does it? It crawls in the dirt on the ground, or at most, up a few plants. And it eats lots of leaves. In fact, too many caterpillars chewing on one plant can kill the plant. Some kinds of caterpillars we don't want in our gardens, because they can ruin what's growing there.

But there's one nice thing about this caterpillar. Can you guess what this is? *(Pause for response.)* Yes, it's going to become a butterfly. It will make a cocoon and later come out as a butterfly [like this one].

A butterfly is completely different from a caterpillar,

isn't it? It doesn't have to grub around in the dirt; it can fly. It doesn't ruin any plants by eating leaves. Instead, it flits from flower to flower, and even helps some flowers in certain ways. And it's so pretty, it brings a touch of beauty wherever it goes.

If you had your choice, what would you rather be, a caterpillar or a butterfly? *(Pause for response.)* I think I'd rather be a butterfly, too.

God wants us to be like butterflies rather than caterpillars. The Bible tells us to put off our old selves and put on a new self. When it talks about our old selves, it means the way we are without Jesus. Our new selves should be the way we become after we know him.

We're all naturally rather like caterpillars. We're not always very nice. We tend to get angry at some people, or jealous of others. We're often very selfish, and we're not always good to people around us.

But we can change. We can use Jesus as our cocoon, wrap ourselves up in him. We can listen to what he has to say and become what he wants us to be.

How does Jesus want us to act? He wants us to be kind, loving, forgiving, gentle. What else can you think of? *(Pause for response.)* That's right, Jesus wants us to be all those things. And when we are, we're like lovely little butterflies.

So don't be a caterpillar Christian. Put off that old, angry, jealous, selfish self. Put on your new self—loving, kind, helpful—and be a butterfly for Jesus.

33

Dead to the World

Scripture: "The man who loves his life will lose it, while the man who hates his life in this world will keep it for eternal life" (John 12:25).

Theme: We should not let things of this world distract us, but focus our attention on Jesus.

Object: A few dead stalks with flowers still atop them, preferably with the seeds intact.

I brought a few flowers with me today; it looks like there's something wrong with them. *(Show the stalks.)* A few days ago, they were like all the other [daisies, Queen Anne's lace, dandelions or whatever you have] growing near them. The flowers were open nice and wide, the plants soaked up the sunlight and they grew a bit when it rained. But then they seemed to lose interest in the sun and rain. They began to shrivel up, and here they are. What's wrong with them? *(Pause for response.)* That's right, they're dead. Sun and rain aren't going to do anything for them now. They're just plain dead to the world.

But that's not bad. That's exactly how it should be. These flowers should be dead to the world.

You see, these flowers were created to help the [kind of flower] plant make seeds. When the seeds begin to form, the flowers must die. They have to forget about the sun and rain, and concentrate on making those seeds. So parts of the flower look like they're dead to the world, but inside, healthy seeds are growing. Finally, the dead parts of the flower fall off *(Rub some of the flower heads to release the seeds.)*, and out come the seeds to grow healthy new plants.

Did you know that Jesus said we should be somewhat like these flowers? He talked about wheat. Wheat plants make seeds the same way this [kind of flower] does. Jesus reminded us that the flower *must* die so that the seeds can grow. And then he said that whoever loses their life for his sake will find it.

Jesus didn't mean that we all should die for him. But he did mean that like these flowers, we should be dead to the world in some ways. We should concentrate on *him,* rather than things around us.

There are lots of things around that can grab our attention. There are always new toys and games out, new clothes, Walkman, skateboards, [whatever happens to be the latest fad], all sorts of things. And all these *things* take a little bit of our attention away from Jesus.

Jesus wants us to be dead to these things. Just like the sun and rain has no effect on these dead flowers *(Show flower stalks.)*, so things of the world shouldn't affect us. Then we can concentrate on the things inside us and what really counts *(Rub another flower to show more seeds.)*: our life with Jesus.

34

God Is in Control

Scripture: And we know that in all things God works for the good of those who love him: (Rom. 8:28).

Theme: God will take the undesirable events of your life and make them work for your good.

Objects: A shoe box with dirt spread on the bottom. On top of the dirt place a few dead leaves, a rotten apple, a dead fish, a dead fly, and a spider. (You can place almost anything on top of the dirt, as long as it's something that most people don't like, and that will eventually decompose. What you put in the box determines exactly what you will say during the first part. This lesson is written with the suggested objects in mind.)

I've got my "yuk box" with me today. I call it my "yuk box" because most people say *yuk* at a lot of the things I have in it. Would you like to see inside? *(Nod your head and smile as you say this to elicit the right response.)* Who will volunteer? *(Give the box to a volunteer.)* Tell us one yukky thing that you see. *(From here on, the order that you take these things depends on the order that they're named.)*

A rotten apple. It doesn't look very good, does it? You certainly wouldn't want to eat it.

Who else would like to take a peek? *(Take the box from*

the first child and give it to another volunteer.) Tell us another thing that's in the box. *(Continue this until all the objects in the box have been identified. After each object is named, give a little comment about how "yukky" we think it is, and then pass the box to another child.)*

A dead fish. It smells a little bad, doesn't it? Fish are okay swimming in some water, or maybe even fried and on our dinner plates, but a rotten, smelly one is yukky.

A few dead leaves. They're not really very bad are they? But still, there's not much you can do with dead leaves. In fact, we rake them off our lawns and sweep them off the sidewalks. They always seem so messy.

Some dirt. That's okay in its place, as long as we don't track it in the house or get it on our clothes. The problem with dirt is that it always seems to creep into places we don't want it.

A spider. Some people like spiders better dead than alive. I think that they're afraid of spiders. Sometimes they don't even want to touch a dead one.

A dead fly. Flies are yukky to us all right, both dead and alive. They have lots of germs on their bodies, and we don't want those germs anywhere near us.

I'll take my yuk box back now because I want to tell you something special about it. *(Take the box from the last volunteer.)* This really isn't a yuk box at all, even though we don't like the things we find in it. This is really a good box.

If I would take this box and put it away some place, just the way it is now, all the things in it probably would get more and more rotten. Finally they'd just fall apart. But you know what would happen then? All the little bits of vitamins and minerals that are stored up in these yukky things would sink into the dirt at the bottom of the box. And that would make the dirt very rich and good for growing food.

That's the way God made the world. We may think there are some yukky or not very good things, but when you take them all together, they turn out to be good.

84

That's the way God makes your life, too. Sometimes things may happen that you think are not good at all. Maybe you have a fight with your best friend, or your family moves and you have to leave your friends. Maybe you have a lot of trouble with a certain subject in school or you're always the last one to be chosen for games. None of these things seem good, do they? They can hurt and make you sad. You'd rather do without them and you wonder why God will let these things happen to you.

But God has said that all things will work together for the good of those who love him. When you fight with a friend, you may learn to be more forgiving; moving away can bring you new friends you would never have known. If you find a school subject hard to understand, you learn how to work hard at something, a little bit at a time. And even being the last one to be chosen for something can help you understand that poor, shy person that no one ever seems to notice. All these things together are really helping to make you a better person, more like God wants you to be.

So when things happen to you that you think aren't very good, remember the yuk box. Nothing in here seems good, but everything's going to work together to make a good, rich soil. In the same way, God's going to take everything that happens to you and make it all work together for your good.

35

Cattail Christians

Scripture: Be devoted to one another in brotherly love. Honor one another above yourselves. Never be lacking in zeal, but keep your spiritual fervor, serving the LORD" (Rom. 12:10, 11).

Theme: It doesn't take special talents or abilities to be a good Christian. We should do what we can, where we are, to show the love of Jesus.

Objects: A bunch of cattails and a rose (or another "flashy" flower).

I've brought a rather strange bouquet of flowers with me today; a bunch of cattails and one beautiful rose. If you were a flower, which would you rather be, one of these cattails or the rose? *(Pause for response.)* Most people would probably like to be the rose.

Let me tell you something about these flowers. Maybe that will change your mind.

This rose may be very pretty, but it's also very fussy. It needs just a certain amount of sunlight and water; it won't grow just anywhere. Besides that, the flowers don't last very long. They're pretty when they're in bloom, but they fade quickly. And everybody knows that roses have thorns.

These cattails aren't especially pretty, but they are very useful. The roots can be cooked and eaten like potatoes, and the stems can be used as a vegetable. The leaves can be woven together to make baskets or even roofs of houses. And these brown things, the flowers, can be eaten when they're young, or ground up and used as baking flour. When these flowers die and this stalk becomes fluffy, that fluffy stuff can be used as stuffing for pillows or sleeping bags. A cattail is far more useful than a rose.

Now what would you rather be, a cattail or a rose? I hope you chose a cattail because I think God wants us to be cattail Christians.

Cattails are more common than roses. Most of us are common, ordinary people, not flashy, like roses. And that's fine; there are lots of good things we can do as cattail Christians.

The Bible points out some things we can do. It says that when others are happy, we should be happy with them. When they're sad, we should *(Pause.)* that's right, be sad with them.

We should share with people in need. If someone is hungry, we should *(Pause.)* feed them. If they're thirsty, we should *(Pause.)* give them something to drink.

We shouldn't fight but should live in *(Pause.)* peace with everyone. We shouldn't hate people, we should *(Pause.)* love them. We should hate what is evil and love what is *(Pause.)* good. We shouldn't think of ourselves first, we should think of *(Pause.)* others.

It doesn't take a flashy, talented person to do those things, does it? It takes a common, ordinary, good-hearted person. If we have the love of Jesus in our hearts, we can do those things.

You don't have to be a supertalented person with all sorts of special abilities to be a good Christian. You don't have to be a rose. Think of the cattails and simply do what you can—where you are—to show the love of Jesus to others. Try to be a good cattail Christian.

36

Stick Tight to God

Scripture: "But be very careful to love the LORD your God to hold fast to him and to serve him with all your heart and all your soul" (Josh. 22:5).

Theme: Hold onto God as tightly as you can.

Object: Sandburs, sticktights, or any kind of dried seeds that stick to clothing.

Note: A piece of Velcro can also be used. (You will have to change the first part of the lesson.)

I picked up some sticktights [sandburs] this week. *(Show them the seeds.)* By the time I had gathered this handful, I wasn't sure whether I had them or they had me. They stick so tightly to whatever touches them.

Watch this. *(Take the sticktights and rub them onto your clothes so that they stay where you put them.)* Once they're stuck on your clothes, they seem to hang on for dear life. These seeds will stick tight, no matter what I do. *(Walk around a bit or shake your clothes to show the seeds sticking tight.)* They can even go through the washing machine and come out still sticking to your clothes!

They have a special way of hanging on—of sticking tight. You can't see it, but these sticktights *(Pull one off your clothes and hold it out.)* have lots of built-in, tiny, tiny hooks. Those hooks catch on your clothes, and that's what makes the seed stick tight to you. Each seed has many, many hooks—many, many ways of sticking tight. *(Put the seed back on your clothes, a bit separate from the other seeds.)*

See the way this seed is sticking tight to me? That's exactly the way we should stick tight to God. The Bible tells us that we should hold fast to God. That's like sticking tight to him.

Just like this seed has many hooks, we have many ways that we can hold fast, or stick tight to God. Try to think of some ways. What can you do to stick tight to God? *(Pause for response.)*

I'll help you with a few. We can pray, can't we? We can talk to God every day and ask him to hold us close. What else can we do? *(Pause for response. Give the following suggestions only if response is not forthcoming or to guide the responses.)* We can read the Bible, remember our Bible stories, obey God's laws, remember his promises, believe in Jesus, love God, love our neighbors, try to serve [live for] God, avoid evil, think about God, remember that God is always with us [and so forth].

All these things that we can do are like little hooks that help us stay close to God, or stick tight to him. The more little hooks we use—the more things we do like pray *(Mention a few they have suggested.)*—the closer we can stay to God. And then nothing will ever separate us from him. *(Take the seed off slowly as you are talking.)*

37

He Cares for You

Scripture: "Are not five sparrows sold for two pennies? Yet not one of them is forgotten by God. Indeed the very hairs of your head are all numbered. Don't be afraid; you are worth more than many sparrows" (Luke 12:6, 7).

Theme: God cares about every little detail in your life.

Object: A feather from a bird. The feather should be large enough for all the children to see it when you hold it up and should zip and unzip rather easily (see below).

I picked up this feather a few days ago, and have been having some fun with it ever since. I love to make it look ragged and then zip it back together again. *(Run your fingers down the feather the wrong way, so that the individual barbs separate from each other; then run your fingers up the feather so that the barbs connect again.)* Have you ever tried that with a feather? You can unzip it and then zip it back together again. *(Demonstrate a few times.)*

God made birds' feathers very special. They really are like little zippers. Each piece of this feather that sticks out from the "stem" has hundreds of tiny hooks on it. This whole feather has thousands of hooks so little that you can't see them. Some reach down, and some reach up. *(Demonstrate by holding your hands out, palms facing, with upper fingers curved downward and lower fingers curved upward.)* When you run your fingers up the feather the right way, or when a bird runs its beak up the feather, all the hooks catch each other *(Catch your fingers together.)* and zip the feather together. Then the feather helps keep the bird warm and dry.

Do you think God cares for his birds? *(Nod your head to elicit the right response.)* It certainly seems like he does. He took a lot of care in the way he made their feathers.

I *know* he cares for his birds. The Bible tells us that God knows when one sparrow falls. He didn't just create the birds and then let them fend for themselves. He watches them so closely all the time that he knows when one little bird falls. He must be constantly watching his birds.

That should make us feel very loved and very cared for. Do you know why? Because God said that he cares for us much more than he cares for his birds. "You are worth more than many sparrows," he said. If he's constantly watching his birds, certainly he's constantly watching over *you.*

He didn't just create you and then forget about you. He is so interested in you that he knows every detail of your life. He's even said that he knows how many hairs you have on your head. And he loves you so much that he watches over you every minute of your life. He was with you when you got up this morning. He's here with you right now, and when you go home, he'll go with you. And he'll always watch you with love and concern.

What more can you ask? This wonderful God, who created the birds just right and constantly watches each one, says that you are much more important to him than many birds. He cares about every little detail in your life, and he will always be with you.

As you leave church today, you can go knowing that God walks with you, and will always be there.

38

Color-blind to the World

Scripture: So we fix our eyes not on what is seen, but on what is unseen. For what is seen is temporary, but what is unseen is eternal (2 Cor. 4:18).

Theme: We should not let things of this world distract us.

Object: A blaze-orange article of clothing such as a hunter's vest or cap.

This vest [cap] is blaze-orange for a very important reason. Can anyone tell me why? *(Pause for response.)* That's right, it's to keep whoever wears it safe.

When someone goes deer hunting, he wears this blaze-orange vest. Other hunters nearby will see the bright color and will be careful when they shoot their guns or their arrows. This color is so bright, it almost screams. You can't miss seeing it.

But deer can miss it. They're color-blind. They don't see this blaze orange. This color blends with everything else, as far as they're concerned. They don't need to see blaze-orange, except maybe to stay away from hunters, so their eyes simply are not created to see it.

Deer *do* need to see movement. They must know when an enemy is nearby. So as any hunter can tell you, their eyes are very sharp when it comes to movement.

Any slight movement will attract a deer's attention. *(Demonstrate as you're talking.)*

Imagine that! They don't see this blaze orange, but they do notice a tiny movement. God gave deer exactly the kind of eyes they need for their life in the woods.

God wants us also to have exactly the kind of eyes we need for our life with him. Not these eyes. *(Point to your eyes.)* He wants us to have special make-believe eyes in our hearts. Let me explain that.

God said that we should not fix our eyes on the things that we see around us. That means we shouldn't set our *hearts* on things that we see around us. We shouldn't want more toys and more clothes, nicer houses, and prettier things.

Instead God said we should fix our eyes on things we *can't* see. We should set our hearts on things that we can't see—like loving people, being good, staying close to God, and believing in Jesus. Those are the things that count. The make-believe eyes in our hearts should be looking at the things that count.

A deer is color-blind to this blaze-orange. We should be color-blind in our hearts to all these things around us that scream for attention. They should not matter at all to us.

A deer is sensitive to the slightest movement. And we should be sensitive to our life with God. That should be the most important thing in the world to us.

39

Palm Sunday

Scripture: John 12:12–15
And my God will meet all your needs according to his glorious riches in Christ Jesus (Phil. 4:19).

Theme: Just as the Israelites depended on palms to meet their everyday needs and for use in celebrations, so we depend on God through Christ to meet our needs, and celebrate eternal life through Jesus.

Objects: A palm plant or a branch of one.

Optional: A coconut and some dates.

Note: Time can determine how many characteristics of palms you want to list. Several are given below.

Today is a special Sunday. Does anyone know what Sunday it is? *(Pause for response.)* That's right, it's Palm Sunday. Today we remember that time, long ago, when Jesus rode into Jerusalem on a donkey, and crowds of Jews welcomed him by waving palm branches.

We don't know exactly what kind of palms they waved. Maybe it was like this. *(Show the palm.)* Maybe it was different. There are many different kinds of palms, so we can't be sure. But we can be sure that the palms the Jews used were special to them.

You see, palms *are* special plants. They always have

been. They were probably the most important plant to grow in Israel when Jesus lived there. They could supply the Jews with everything they needed for everyday life.

For food the Israelites often ate dates. *(Pass the dates around.)* These come from palm trees. The Israelites also squeezed the dates and drank the juice. So those "trees" could supply the Israelites both food and drink.

(Optional, if you have a coconut.) Coconuts come from palms too. *(Pass the coconut[s] around.)* Everybody knows that coconuts are good to eat. And if you squeeze them, you get coconut milk. So again you can see, palm trees supplied the Israelites with both food and drink.

Palms also provided shelter for the Israelites. They would often take these leaves *(Show the fronds.)*, tie them together, and use them for the roofs of their houses.

Some palms can grow where there is very little water and very hot temperatures. Israelites traveling in the desert near Jerusalem often looked eagerly for palm trees. They knew that there they would find at least a little water, and there they could rest in the shade of the palms. The Israelites depended on palms for shelter from the weather.

They even used palms in their everyday affairs. Feel these fronds. *(Let the children run their hands over the fronds.)* Can you feel how tough and stringy they are? The Israelites used to take these fronds and weave them together for ropes, baskets, sandals, and even mats like carpets.

You can see that palms were very important to the Israelites, so it was natural for them to welcome Jesus to Jerusalem by waving palm branches.

Now a palm branch is a perfect symbol or sign for Jesus, isn't it? Think about it for a minute. People depended on palms for life. We depend on Jesus for eternal life. Palms could supply all the people's needs. God said that he will supply all *our* needs through Christ Jesus. People used palm branches in celebrations. And because of Jesus, we can celebrate God's victory over sin.

Since today is Palm Sunday, you may hear people talking about palms just a little more, or you may see some more palm branches. And now you know just how important palms can be. But all through the year, when you see a palm [or look at this palm in front of church], you can think about how it stands for Jesus. And then you can remember that Jesus can supply all your needs and came to give you eternal life.

40

Crown of Thorns (Good Friday)

Scripture: But he was pierced for our transgressions, he was crushed for our iniquities; the punishment that brought us peace was upon him, and by his wounds we are healed (Isa. 53:5).

. . . and then wove a crown of thorns and set it on his head: (Matt. 27:29).

Theme: Jesus underwent very real, physical suffering for us.

Objects: A few stems from a thorny plant. Crown of thorns plant is best, but may be rather difficult to obtain. Stems from a barberry plant or any bramble patch (or raspberry patch) are good. Stems from roses (with the thorns still intact) will do. Take a few stems, soak them in water to make them pliable, and make a crown of thorns. A bag of nails and a hammer.

For a little while let's pretend that a new law was just passed in our city [county, state], and it affects you. That's right; it's against the law now to be a kid. Anyone that's younger than twelve years old (*Or at least a year older than the oldest child there.*) is supposed to be punished, just for being a kid. That's what this pretend law calls for.

This is the punishment. (*Show them the crown of*

thorns.) You're supposed to wear something like this, jammed down on your head, for at least an hour every day if you're under twelve years old.

I made this last night, just to show you what you could be in for. This thing is full of thorns, and I can tell you that it hurt just to make it. My fingers bled a little, and I got a few thorns under my skin that are still there bothering me. I'm glad I don't have to wear it; it's going to hurt.

I'll pass this around so that you can get a closer look at it. *(Pass the crown of thorns around.)* You don't have to wear it yet; just take a look at it. But handle it carefully; those thorns can rip your skin.

There's more to the law than that. It also says that, if you continue to be a kid, even after you've worn those thorns, you've got to suffer more. You have to be nailed down in place for a while, so that you won't run around like kids do. *(Show them the nails and hammer.)* Someone's got to hammer these through your hands and feet to nail you against a wall or pieces of wood so that you won't move.

Pretty awful, isn't it? But that's what this suppose law says. You're all kids, so you're going to have to pay. Who would like to be the first one, either with the thorns or the nails? No volunteers? I don't blame you.

There is a way out of this. The law also says that some adult can take your place. So if I wanted to, I could put those thorns on my head, and let someone nail me against a wall. Then you *all* could go free.

Maybe I can take the thorns; let me try. *(Take the crown of thorns and put it gently on your head.)* That hurts, and I don't even have it jammed down all the way yet. I don't think I can keep it on for an hour. I know I can't stand being nailed against a wall; that's too awful. I'm sorry, but I can't do it for you. Looks like you're each going to have to take your own punishment. *(Take off the crown of thorns.)* You know, of course, I'm pretending about that new law. There's no law that says you can't be a kid. That would be an impossible law to keep.

But there *is* a law that we're all under, that *is* impossible to keep. It's God's law. He says that we may not sin. Because God is perfect, he can't stand sin and he says that sin must be punished. But we all sin, don't we? We can't help it because we're sinful. So we must be punished.

But there is a way out, just like there was a way out of our imaginary law. Who knows what that way is? *(Pause for response.)* That's right; Jesus is the way out.

Jesus already took all the punishment for us. He did wear a crown of thorns like this, jammed down on his head, for many hours. He was nailed up for us, with nails like these through his hands and feet. And he died and was even separated from God for us. We don't know what it's like to be separated from God. It's got to be much worse than these thorns and nails. It's got to be the most awful thing you can ever imagine. Yet Jesus loved us so much, he did it for us, to pay the price for our sins.

So now when we talk about Jesus' suffering and dying for our sins, think about these thorns and these nails and how they would feel. And you'll have just a little bit of an idea of how Jesus suffered for us. Then say with your whole heart, "Thank you, Jesus."

41

You Are the Lily
(Easter)

Scripture: But Christ has indeed been raised from the dead, the firstfruits of those who have fallen asleep. For as in Adam all die, so in Christ all will be made alive (1 Cor. 15:20, 22).

Theme: Christ died for us and rose again so that we could live, blameless, forever with him.

Objects: An Easter lily, a lily bulb, and a pot of dirt.

You all know what this is, don't you? *(Show them the lily.)* Who can tell me? *(Pause for response.)* That's right, it's an Easter lily. People like to use it this time of year to decorate for Easter. They say that the lily reminds them of new life through Jesus.

But I have something here that can remind us of Jesus even more than this plant. *(Show them the lily bulb.)* This is called a *lily bulb*. You don't often see one because it is usually buried in dirt. But this is what the lily plant grows from. If we don't have a lily bulb, we can't have a lily.

This bulb looks dead, doesn't it? It might as well be dead right now. It's not going to do anything sitting in my hand. It has to be buried to grow into a lily.

That's why I think this bulb can remind us of Jesus.

He had to die to save us from our sins. And he had to be buried to show that he was really dead. *(Take the bulb and bury it in the pot of dirt.)*

There. Now I've buried the bulb. In a few days it will come to life. Then you'll be able to see a little lily growing up out of the dirt.

That's like what happened to Jesus, isn't it? Jesus was really dead and buried. But three days later he came back to life. He came out of his grave alive to prove that God is stronger than death. Because he died and rose again, we can live with him forever.

(Direct their attention to the potted lily.) This plant is growing from a lily bulb. These stems and leaves are alive because a bulb was buried but is alive down there where you can't see it.

You're like this plant. You're alive and can live forever with Jesus because he, like the bulb, is alive. In fact, to God, you even look like these beautiful white flowers. There's not a spot on them, is there? And there's not a spot of sin on you, because Jesus took your sins away.

Therefore this lily can remind you of Easter. You can look at the stems and leaves and know that you have life through Jesus. You can look at the white flower and know that you have no sin because of Jesus. But don't forget that bulb, living where you can't see it right now. That stands for Jesus, who died, was buried, came back to life, and is living right now so that you can live forever with God.

42

He's Coming Again (Ascension Day)

Scripture: ". . . This same Jesus, who has been taken from you into heaven, will come back in the same way you have seen him go into heaven" (Acts 1:11).

Theme: Jesus physically ascended into heaven and will return some day.

Object: A helium-filled balloon.

Can anyone tell me what special day we're going to celebrate this week? *(Pause for response.)* That's a hard question. Sometimes even adults forget about this day. This Thursday is going to be Ascension Day.

That's a long word. Does anyone know what it means? *(Pause for response.)* Ascension means "going up." *(Gesture upward.)* Thursday will be the day when we especially remember that Jesus ascended—went up into heaven.

You've probably heard the story already. About six weeks after Jesus rose from the dead, he took his disciples to a hill near Jerusalem. As he was standing there talking to them, he simply floated up from the ground into the sky. The disciples watched him go, until a cloud hid him from their view.

That never happens, does it? A person doesn't just

float from the ground up into the sky. But it happened to Jesus. He ascended, or went up—body and all—into heaven.

Right after the cloud hid him, angels came down and talked to his disciples. They told the disciples that Jesus had gone to heaven. They also said that someday he would come back to earth again, the same way that he went to heaven.

So we know that, someday, Jesus will come back to earth, in the body that he had while he was here before. God promised us that through those angels. And meanwhile Jesus is in heaven with that body.

Sometimes it's hard to remember all that, because we can't see Jesus in his body right now. We know that he's in heaven and we know that he will come back. But we tend to forget, because we don't see him.

So I've brought something to help us remember. (Show them the balloon.)

What will happen to this balloon if I let go of the string? (*Pause for response.*) That's right, it will float up to the ceiling. This balloon can help us remember Jesus. (*Let the balloon go.*) Just like it's going up to the ceiling, Jesus ascended into heaven.

Will the balloon stay up there forever? (*Pause for response.*) No! Gradually the gas will leak out, and it will come down. I'm not sure when. Maybe today, maybe sometime during the week. But it will come down— that's for sure.

More sure than that is the fact that Jesus will come again. God has promised us.

You can look at the balloon once in a while today, while it's up there. And that can remind you that Jesus ascended, went up to heaven, body and all. If it comes down during this service, you'll be reminded that Jesus is coming again.

But we don't know when he'll come—just as we don't know when the balloon will come down. If it's still up there when we leave today, that will give you some-

103

thing to think about all week. And especially this Thursday, you can remember that Jesus ascended into heaven and is coming again.

43

Filled with the Spirit (Pentecost)

Scripture: "The wind blows wherever it pleases. You hear its sound, but you cannot tell where it comes from or where it is going. So it is with everyone born of the Spirit" (John 3:8).

Theme: Although we can't see the Holy Spirit, we can see evidences of his presence.

Objects: Three balloons and a dark, broad-tipped indelible marker. Blow up the balloons ahead of time so that you know they will inflate easily. While they are filled take the marker and print PETER on one of them. On the second draw a big heart. Inside the heart print LOVE, KINDNESS and THE STORY OF JESUS. Leave the third balloon blank. Let the air out of the balloons, but be sure they can be easily inflated.

This is a very special Sunday. Today we celebrate the time that Jesus sent the Holy Spirit to his disciples. So we're going to talk about the Holy Spirit today.

Can you see the Spirit? *(Shake your head to elicit the right response.)* Of course not. Jesus said that the Spirit is like the wind; you can't see him, but you can see where he's working.

It's hard to think and talk about something you can't see, isn't it? Maybe this will help. I'm going to blow, and I want you to try to watch the air I'm blowing. *(Blow into the air a few times.)* Can you see my air? Can you see where it went? Of course not; you can't see air. *(Take out the unmarked balloon.)*

Now let's try again. *(Blow up the balloon and hold it up.)* You still can't see my air, but can you see where it is? *(Point to the balloon.)* Yes, it's in the balloon. Now watch; can you see what my air is doing? *(Let the balloon go.)* It's pushing [or it pushed] the balloon around.

That's what Jesus meant when he talked about the Spirit. You can't see him, but you can see where he is—you can tell when someone is filled with the Spirit—and you can see how the Spirit works.

When the Holy Spirit filled the disciples, everybody around them saw his work.

Jesus had gone to heaven and the disciples felt scared and lonely. Even Peter, who always was so bold, just sat in a room with the rest of the disciples. *(Take out the balloon marked PETER.)* He was rather like this balloon. He couldn't really do anything or tell anybody about Jesus all by himself. He didn't know what to do. But then Jesus sent the Holy Spirit, who filled the disciples. *(Blow up the balloon.)* And Peter stood up and told the story of Jesus to a whole crowd of people who had gathered. The other disciples stood up and talked too. And about three thousand people became Christians that day, because the Holy Spirit had come and worked in the disciples and in them. *(Let the air out of the balloon slowly.)*

That happened long ago. Do you think the Holy Spirit still works today? *(Pause for response.)* Of course! He can work in us the very same way he worked in the disciples. *(Take out the other marked balloon.)*

We're a lot like the disciples were. We know that Jesus died to save us, and that he wants us to tell others about him. We know that he wants us to be good and kind and to love each other. But sometimes it's hard to do all that by ourselves. We're just like this balloon. We may have

106

love and kindness and the story of Jesus written in our hearts, but we don't know how to let it show. But if we ask the Holy Spirit to come into our lives, he will fill us and work through us. *(Blow up the balloon.)* He helps us show kindness and love and tell others about Jesus. He's the power that can help us and be with us wherever we go. *(Let the balloon fly.)*

There's a big difference between the air in those balloons and the Holy Spirit. Look at the balloons; they're all down. They ran out of air. The Holy Spirit never runs out of power because he's *God*. He can be with you all the time and wherever you go. So you never need to be afraid or shy. Ask the Holy Spirit to come and fill you, and he'll help you talk about Jesus and show his love.

44

The Meaning of Christmas

Scripture: ". . . I have come that they may have life, and have it to the full" (John 10:10).

Theme: Jesus was born to give us eternal life.

Object: A Christmas tree (if you have one in church) or an evergreen bough. (If you have a tree in church and the children come to the front, have them sit around the tree.)

I brought a little piece of a Christmas tree with me today so that we could talk about it. [Or, I wanted you to sit near the tree today, so that we could talk about it.] Did you know that even before a Christmas tree is decorated, it's something very special? It is. Let's see if you can figure out why it's special.

Is this tree dead or alive? [Or, if the tree is artificial, does this tree *look* dead or alive?] *(Pause for response.)* Yes, it's alive. [Or, *it's made to look like it's alive.*]

How do you know? *(Pause for response.)* Because it's green. Dead trees are never green, are they? They're brown.

If you went outside right now and looked at some trees, would they all be green? *(Pause. The answer you receive and what you say next will depend on your section of the country.)* Of course not! In fact, some trees look like they're dead right now, don't they?

But the Christmas trees don't. These trees stay green all year. That's what makes a Christmas tree so special—even before it's decorated. When everything around it looks dead, this tree looks like it's brimming over with life.

And that's why we often use this special tree at Christmas. Christmas is after all a very special holiday, isn't it? Whose birthday do we remember? *(Pause.)* Yes, Jesus'! This is the time of year that we celebrate the fact that Jesus came to earth as a little baby.

Why did he come? *(Pause.)* That's right; he came to save us from our sins. The Bible says that once we were dead in sin. That doesn't mean our bodies were dead. That means we were dead inside; our souls [or spirits] were dead. But Jesus came to take our sins away and make us alive inside again. He said that he came so that we could have life. And if we believe in him, we can live forever with him. We will never again die inside.

You could almost say that we would be like little Christmas trees. Although there's sin and death in the world, just like those brown trees without leaves, we can always be alive and healthy inside with God.

So now when you see a Christmas tree or any evergreen tree, you don't have to think of decorations, or presents, or tinsel, do you? You can look at that nice, green tree, brimming with life, and think of the full, eternal life that Jesus brought you.

45

To Remember Him
(Communion)

Scripture: And he took bread, gave thanks and broke it,
and gave it to them, saying, "This is my body given for
you; do this in remembrance of me" (Luke 22:19).

Theme: Christians take communion to remember Jesus'
sacrifice for us.

Object: A few slices of bread (enough so each child can
have a small piece).

Note: You will have to adjust the last part of this lesson to
suit communion in your church.

I brought a few slices of bread with me today.
I'm going to pass them around. I want each of you to
tear off just a little bit and keep it for yourself. *(Pass the
bread and wait until all the children have a small piece.)* Do
you all have some? Now I want you to eat it slowly.

Long ago Jesus did this same thing with his disciples.
He passed some bread to them and told them to eat it.
While they were eating it, he said that it was his body.

Do you think he meant that his disciples were really
eating his body? *(Pause for response.)* No. He meant that
the bread should *remind* them of his body.

Just like the bread was broken *(Break up a bit of bread
while you are talking.),* so Jesus' body was torn and

bruised and nailed to a cross. When you eat bread, it helps keep you alive. And when you believe that Jesus died on a cross, your soul can live forever with him. So Jesus meant that eating the broken bread can remind us of him.

When he gave his disciples the bread Jesus said, "Do this in remembrance of me." We believe that Jesus wanted all of his followers to do that.

So that's what we're going to do here today. When you see the adults passing communion bread and eating it, you'll know that they're doing that to show that they remember Jesus and believe in him. That's what Jesus told us to do.

The adults will also pass little cups of wine [grape juice] and drink them. Jesus told us to do that too, to remember that he bled for our sins.

I'm not going to give you anything to drink here. I think the bread was enough to show you what it is all about.

But soon you will see both bread and wine [juice] passed. Then you can remember the bread that you ate up here. But most important, you too can remember that Jesus died for your sins.

46

Pray Without Ceasing (Prayer Day)

Scripture: Pray continually; give thanks in all circumstances, for this is God's will for you in Christ Jesus (1 Thess. 5:17, 18).

". . . I tell you the truth, my Father will give you whatever you ask in my name" (John 16:23).

Theme: We should be in constant prayer to God.

Object: A praying mantis, or a picture of one.

Can anyone tell me what type of insect this is? *(Pause.)* That's right, it's a praying mantis. Can you guess what I'm going to talk about today? *(Pause.)* Prayer!

I thought that this praying mantis would be a good example because it looks like it's always praying. The Bible tells us that we should pray continually, or all the time. So, when you see a praying mantis, you can remember that you should be praying, too.

Since God told us to pray all the time, should we *always* have our hands folded, our eyes closed, and be sitting very still? *(Pause for response.)* Of course not! God expects us to eat and sleep, work, and play. We can't do all that with our hands folded and our eyes closed.

You can pray without folding your hands and closing your eyes. You can talk to God anytime, no matter what you're doing. Even when you're walking to school, you can say "God, help me in school today." Or when you're playing with a friend, you can think, "God, help me to be good to my friend." God will hear you, even if you don't have your hands folded and your eyes closed.

There's something a little strange about our praying mantis. Do you think this bug is really praying? *(Pause for response.)* Of course not. Bugs don't pray. It just looks like it's praying because it sits with its front feet together. So it's really a fake, isn't it?

Do you think God wants us to fake our prayers to him? *(Pause for response.)* No! When God tells us to pray, he wants us to truly talk to him, not to fake it.

So in a way, we should be just opposite from this praying mantis, shouldn't we? This looks like it's always praying, but it never really is. We can't sit and look like we're praying all the time—we *should* always be talking to God.

You can go back to your seats now. And maybe you can say a little prayer as you go.

47

Seeds of Heaven
(Mission Sunday)

Scripture: Luke 8:11–15
". . . The seed is the word of God" (Luke 8:11).

Theme: We should share the good news of Jesus with others.

Object: A packet of corn seeds (any seeds will do, but corn seeds are best).

I have some wonderful seeds with me today—corn seeds. How many of you like corn on the cob? *(Pause for response.)* I thought so; almost everybody likes it. Would you like some of my corn when it's grown? *(Nod to elicit the right response.)* Okay. When it's ripe, I'll bring it to church. That way I can share my corn with you.

Wait a minute! That's going to be a long time from now. Do you think I'll really be able to share my corn with you? What if I'm out of town when the corn is ripe? Or, what if I bring it to church and you're not here that day? How can we be absolutely certain that I can share this corn? *(Pause for response. Answer the responses to show the improbability of all of them eating from your garden, such as, "Suppose I'm not home when you come to get it?" "Suppose you don't know where my garden is?" "Sup-*

pose I move away before the corn is grown?") I have an idea. I think each of you should have your own corn patch. Then you'll all be able to eat corn.

So here's how I'm going to share my corn with you. I'm going to give you some seeds to plant. Then you can grow your own corn from my seeds. *(Pass out the seeds.)* There! Now you all have your own seeds.

You really have two kinds of seeds. They're not both corn seeds. You have corn seeds in your hand but other seeds in your heart.

Did you know that you have seeds in your heart? They're not really seeds, they're much better than corn seeds. But we can call them *seeds—seeds of heaven.*

Let me try to explain that. How many of you know who Jesus is? Raise your hand if you do. Keep your hand up if you know that he's God's Son who came to die for your sins. If you know that good news about Jesus, then you have seeds of heaven in your heart.

If you believe in your heart that Jesus is God's Son and he died for your sins, and you try to stay near him all your life, then your love for Jesus will grow, just as a corn plant will grow from this seed. And when you die, you'll go to heaven to live with Jesus.

There are some people who won't go to heaven. They don't have a chance, because they don't have those seeds of heaven in their hearts. They don't know the good news about Jesus. They can't grow to love him, because they don't even know him. So they can't go to heaven to live with him.

That's really sad. Is there something that we can do about that? Think of the corn I shared with you. *(Pause for response.)* That's right. We can *tell* them the good news about Jesus. That's one of the most important things we can do in this life: tell others about Jesus [If applicable.] What else can we do? We can help our missionaries bring the good news to other people. We can pray for our missionaries; we can help support our missionaries, [and so forth]. There are all sorts of ways we

115

can spread the good news about Jesus. That's something you may want to talk to your parents about when you get home today. When we tell others about Jesus, we're sharing those seeds of heaven that we have in our heart.

The good thing about these seeds in our hearts is that they never run out. If I tried to share my corn seeds with everyone in church, I'd probably run out of seeds. But when we tell others about Jesus, we still have him in our hearts. So we can tell the whole world about Jesus and still have our own seeds of heaven.

So you're really holding two types of seeds right now, the corn and the good news about Jesus. Go ahead and plant those corn seeds, but make sure you share those other precious seeds. Make sure others can also hear about Jesus.

48

God's Fruit Salad (Ethnic Diversity)

Scripture: . . . he prophesied that Jesus would die for the Jewish nation, and not only for that nation but also for the scattered children of God, to bring them together and make them one (John 11:51, 52).

Theme: People of many different colors and cultural backgrounds make up the church of Christ.

Object: A fruit salad, containing several different types of fruit, in a clear glass bowl.

I brought along the fruit salad that we're going to have for lunch [supper, dinner] today. I think it's so pretty, with all these different colors, don't you?

(Fashion this according to what fruit you have in the salad. The point is that each fruit has something good to recommend it.) I really like bananas. They're so smooth and have a mellow taste. Sometimes I like to eat just a banana. Oranges are good, too. They're nice and juicy, and can be so sweet. The cherries [or grapes or whatever] can also be sweet by themselves. And the pineapple—sometimes I love the tart taste of pineapple. All of these fruits are perfectly fine by themselves.

But the taste of a fruit salad, I think, is something

special. I guess it's the mixing together of all the fruits that gives this a special taste.

Did you ever think of yourself as a banana? That's a strange thought, isn't it? Let me explain what I mean.

In a way, God's people, taken all together, are like this fruit salad. There are some bananas, Christians like you and me. We all live in ___[town]___, and *(List a few common characteristics of the group.)*. Then there are apples, maybe Christians that live right here in _____, but are a different color, or live a little differently from us. And there are oranges—Christians living in Germany—that speak a different language. And pineapples—Christians living in Borneo—who look different from us speak a language that's strange to us and wear different clothes. Maybe the cherries are Christians who live in China. They're different from all of us. Each group is different, but each group is perfectly fine alone.

Yet, we're all part of God's fruit salad because we are all *Christians*. We all belong to God's people because we all believe in Jesus.

Sometimes, when we're bananas living with a bunch of bananas, we tend to forget that there are apples, oranges, pineapples, and cherries living out there. But all parts of the fruit salad are there, and God never forgets. In fact, the Bible says that Jesus died for the scattered children of God, to bring them together and make them one. He looks at all of us together just as we look at this bowl of fruit salad.

It's good to remember that we're one part of this giant fruit salad. Because when we're mixed together with other Christians, we can all help to bring that special flavor to the world. Together, with other Christians, we all do our part to spread God's Word.

So, you little bananas, you look good to me, and God loves you just the way you are. But when you meet some apples or oranges or maybe even pineapples— Christians different from you—remember that we're all a part of God's fruit salad. Together we all belong to him.

118

49

Share the Wealth (World Hunger)

Scripture: ". . .Whatever you did for one of the least of these brothers of mine, you did for me" (Matt. 25:40).

He who is kind to the poor lends to the LORD, and he will reward him for what he has done (Prov. 19:17).

Theme: We should share with the poor what God has given us.

Object: Treats (grapes, raisins, fruit bits or something similar) for the children. Be sure to bring enough so that each child could have at least one.

Note: This lesson can take many forms, depending on how far you want to guide the children and how much you want to let them work out on their own or discuss with their parents. Use your imagination. A few suggestions are given below.

I brought a little treat for you today. (*Pass out all the treats to the children on your right, so they each have several. Ignore the children on your left, so that they have nothing.*)

Oh, it looks like something went wrong. Some of you don't have any yet, do you? I don't have anymore, but I see that some of you have more than enough.

First Form. What should we do about this? (*Direct the*

119

question to the "haves" and pause for response.) I think that's a good idea. We should share what we have with them.

But before you share, I want all of you to think about something. Pretend for a minute that you stand for all the people of the world. Some people *(Gesture to the "haves.")* have lots of things; plenty of food, lots of clothes, nice, warm houses, more than enough of everything they need. But there are always poor people *(Gesture to the "have nots."),* aren't there? There are people who don't have enough to eat; they're starving. And there are people without good clothes to wear, or houses to live in. The world is like that. There may be enough to go around, but it isn't shared equally. Some people have more than enough and some have nothing.

Who do you think *we* are? Are we the people with more than enough, or are we the poor [the starving]? *(Pause for response.)* That's right, we're the people with more than enough. We have plenty of food [clothes, places to live].

What does God want us to do, since we're the people with plenty? *(Pause for response.)* Yes, he wants us to share with those that don't have enough. In fact, God said that when we share with others, it's just like we're sharing with him. And if we don't share, it's as if we're keeping things from God. God even said that he will reward people who give to the poor.

Sometimes it's hard to share with poor people. Do you know people who are so poor they don't have enough to eat or a place to sleep? Some of us don't; yet we hear about them at times. How can we share with people we don't even know? *(Pause for response.)* There are all sorts of ways we can share. Maybe you should talk about this with your parents when you get home today.

Of course, sharing these treats is easy. We just have to pass them around a bit. So *(To the "haves.")* why don't you share your treats now? You're like the people who

120

have plenty of food, sharing with those who have nothing. *(See that the treats are equally distributed.)*

There. Now that everyone has something, you can go back to your seats. Take the treat along with you, and let it remind you of all the things you have. And when you eat it, try to think of ways that you can share with people who don't have enough. That's what God wants you to do.

Second Form. Oh, well, that's the way it goes. Sorry about that. Life isn't always fair.

You know, that's just the point I wanted to make today. Life doesn't always seem fair. That's the way it is.

We could pretend that you're all the people of the world. Some people *(Gesture to the "haves.")* have more than enough. They have plenty of food, lots of clothes, a good, warm house and all sorts of things. But then, there are always poor people *(Gesture to the "have nots.")*. Some of them are starving for lack of food. Some don't have more than one little rag to wear, and some have no place to sleep.

Who are we, the people who have plenty or poor people? *(Pause for response.)* That's right, we have plenty. We have more than enough food [clothes, homes].

What does God want us to do, since we're the people with plenty? *(Pause for response.)* Yes, he wants us to share with those that don't have enough. In fact God said that when we share what we have with others, it's just like we're giving to him. And if we don't share, it's like we're keeping things from God. God even said that he will reward people who give to the poor.

You can go back to your seats now. But I want you to think about something. You people who don't have a treat, imagine how it feels to have no food when you know there are some people with more than enough. And you people who have treats, think of those who don't have any. Do what you think you should with your treat.

All of you can think about how much we have, and how God wants us to share with others.

Third Form. Oh, well, that's the way it goes. Sorry about that. Life isn't always fair.

You know, that's just the point I wanted to make today. Life doesn't always seem fair. That's the way it is.

We could pretend that you're all the people of the world. Some people *(Gesture to the "haves.")* have more than enough. They have plenty of food, lots of clothes, a good, warm house and all sorts of things. But then there are always poor people *(Gesture to the "have nots.")*. Some of them are starving for lack of food. Some don't have more than one little rag to wear, and some have no place to sleep.

God wants us to share with those that don't have enough. In fact, God said that when we share what we have with others, it's just like we're giving to him. And if we don't share, it's like we're keeping things from God. God even said that he will reward people who give to the poor.

This is a short lesson [message] today. I'm almost finished talking, but I want you to do a lot of thinking. You people who don't have a treat, imagine how it feels to have no food when you know there are some people with more than enough. And you people who have treats, think of those who didn't get any. Do what you think you should with your treat.

All of you can think about how much we have, and how God wants us to share with others.

50

A Death in God's Family

Scripture: Jesus said to her, "I am the resurrection and the life. He who believes in me will live, even though he dies; and whoever lives and believes in me will never die . . ." (John 11:25,26).

Theme: Death is simply the casting off of an earthly body.

Object: The cast-off shell of an insect (or a spider) that has molted or a picture of one. A cicada is very good, since it's big enough for the children to see. A snake skin will do, although not quite as well, as it doesn't retain the shape. Look on the ground in protected places, such a thick vegetation. (If you live near water, you may be able to find a crayfish shell. In a pinch, a lobster shell will do.) If you cannot find one and draw a picture instead, be sure to put a split line up the back, where the creature has crawled out of its skin.

Can you see what I have here? *(Show the shell or picture rather quickly, so the children have the impression of a full-bodied insect or snake.)* It looks like some sort of insect [snake], doesn't it? But look at it more closely. *(Give the children a chance to study the shell or skin.)* Is it really an insect [snake]? *(Pause for response.)* No! It's only the shell [skin].

Some bug [spider, snake] grew too big for its [shell] skin. The skin [shell] split along this little line, the bug [snake] crawled out and flew [walked, slithered] away,

123

leaving the old [shell] skin behind. The bug [snake] was still alive; it simply didn't need this shell [skin] anymore.

Something like that happened to ___[name]___ this week. You've probably all heard that he/she died. There have been a lot of tears, because people will miss him/her. His/her body is dead, and we can't bring it back to life. So we cry—and that's okay—because _____ has left us.

But is _____ really dead? Did that soul, that spirit, that person that was _____ die when his/her body died? *(Pause for response.)* Of course not! Jesus said that whoever believed in him would never die. We know that _____ believed in Jesus, so he/she isn't really dead.

The time just came this week that Jesus said, "_____, I want you in heaven with me. Your time on earth is finished." Suddenly, he/she didn't need his/her earthly body—the thing that we see—anymore. So his/her soul left the body and went to be with Jesus in heaven.

We were left only with the body, rather like this cast-off shell, that _____ didn't need anymore. And we did cry, because we lost the real _____. And then we had a funeral and buried that body that he/she doesn't need.

But although it hurts us to lose someone we love, deep down inside we can celebrate for him/her. We know that now he/she is happy, living with Jesus. And we know that, if we believe in Jesus too, someday we will see _____ again in heaven.

51

God's Valentine to You
(Valentine's Day)

Scripture: "For God so loved the world that he gave his one and only Son, that whoever believes in him shall not perish but have eternal life" (John 3:16).

Theme: God loved us so much that he sent Jesus to die for us.

Objects: A valentine and a picture of Jesus cut into the shape of a heart.

Note: It would be ideal to have a "valentine" of Jesus for each child. This lesson will work with just one Jesus "valentine" if a copier is not available.

I think everybody here could tell me what this is. *(Show them the valentine and pause for response.)* You're right, it's a valentine. We'll see a lot of these this week. ___[Day of week]___ will be Valentine's Day, so lots of people will send and receive valentines.

People often give valentines to just about everybody they know. Sometimes people give them to everyone in their class at school. Maybe you do that too. It's nice to let people know you're thinking about them, and to wish them a happy day.

When we send out a lot of valentines, often we keep the very special ones for people who are really special to us. Maybe you want to let Mom and Dad or a very close friend know that you really do love them. So you pick out a special valentine to send to them. Usually it's extra pretty, and it says something like "I love you." At any rate, it's a special valentine to show love from you to them.

Do you know who sent the most special valentine of all time? *(Pause briefly for response.)* God did! He sent a very, very special valentine from him to you. Here it is. *(Show them the picture of Jesus.)*

Of course, this paper isn't the valentine that God sent you, but it does have a picture of God's valentine. Who is it? *(Pause for response.)* That's right, it's Jesus! Jesus is like God's special valentine to you, only much, much better.

God loved you so much, that he sent Jesus, his only Son, to die for your sins. Nobody can ever love you more than God loves you.

So when you're giving valentines away this week, or when you get them from your friends, stop for a minute and think of God's special valentine to you. He loves you so much that he gave you Jesus.

52

Citizens of Two Countries (Patriotic Holiday)

Scripture: ". . . Has not God chosen those . . . to inherit the kingdom he promised those who love him?" (James 2:5).

Theme: Christians are citizens of their own country and the kingdom of heaven.

Objects: A national flag, a Christian flag, and a Bible.

Note: Suggestions here are for Fourth of July in the USA, but it can be done for a national holiday in any country.

What holiday are we going to celebrate this week? Maybe this will give you a hint. *(Wave the national flag and pause for response.)* That's right, the Fourth of July, the birthday of our country. You'll probably see lots of flags out this week. People like to fly them to show that they're citizens of the USA.

Let's see for a minute what you know about our country. Do we have a president or a king? *(Pause for response.)* That's right, and he's the head of our country. What's his name? *(Pause for response.)* Good. Do we have laws? *(Pause for response.)* Of course, but most of them are to protect us, not to make us do things we don't want to do. This is a free country. We can thank God that we live here. And we can wave fly our flags to show that we're American citizens.

But we're also citizens of another country. Who can tell me what flag this is? *(Show them the Christian flag and pause for response.)* That's right; it's a Christian flag. When we fly this flag, we tell everyone that we are also citizens of the kingdom of heaven. We're not living there yet, but if we're Christians, we know that some-day we will.

We already have a King who's greater than President   [current chief executive]   . Who is our King? *(Pause for response.)* That's right; Jesus is, and we're loyal to him above everyone else. We also have a set of laws and of promises. Where can you find them? *(Show them the Bible and pause for response.)* Sure; in the Bible. The Bible tells us how citizens of heaven should live, and prom-ises us that we will see heaven if we believe in Jesus.

But best of all, the Bible also tells about freedom in heaven. It says that you will be free of tears. You will never cry in heaven because you will never be sad. You'll be free of pain. You'll never get sick, and you'll never even fall down and skin your knees. And you will be free of fear. Are you afraid of the dark now, or maybe of some neighbor's dog? You won't have any fears like that in heaven.

Doesn't heaven sound like a wonderful place to live? If you're a Christian, you will live there someday. If you believe in Jesus, you are already a citizen of heaven.

So have a good time on the Fourth of July. If you have an American flag, fly it. If you have a Christian flag, you could fly that too. Even if you don't, you can remember that you are a citizen of two countries. You live in the USA now, but someday you will live forever in heaven.